PUT ON YOUR OWN OXYGEN MASK FIRST

REDISCOVERING MINISTRY

BILL EASUM

with Linnea Nilsen Capshaw

ABINGDON PRESS / Nashville

PUT ON YOUR OWN OXYGEN MASK FIRST:
REDISCOVERING MINISTRY

Copyright © 2004 by Abingdon Press

All rights reserved.

This book is printed on acid-free paper.

Library of Congress Cataloging-in-Publication Data

Easum, William M., 1939-
Put on your own oxygen mask first : rediscovering ministry / Bill Easum with Linnea Nilsen Capshaw.
p. cm.
ISBN 0-687-00078-5 (binding: adhesive, pbk. : alk. paper)
1. Pastoral theology. 2. Vocation, Ecclesiastical. I. Capshaw, Linnea Nilsen. II. Title.

BV4011.3.E27 2004
253—dc22

2003028147

All Scripture quotations unless noted otherwise are taken from the *New Revised Standard Version of the Bible*, copyright 1989, by the Division of Christian Education of the National Council of the Churches of Christ in the United States of America. Used by permission. All rights reserved.

Scripture quotations marked (NIV) are taken from the HOLY BIBLE, NEW INTERNATIONAL VERSION®. Copyright © 1973, 1978, 1984 by International Bible Society. Used by permission of Zondervan Publishing House. All rights reserved.

Scripture quotations marked KJV are from the King James or Authorized Version of the Bible.

Chapter 9 chart on page 102 is adapted from an exercise designed by Thomas Bandy. Used by permission.

Appendix 3 articles reprinted by permission, *Rev. Magazine*, Copyright 2003, Group Publishing, Inc., Box 481, Loveland, CO 80539.

04 05 06 07 08 09 10 11 12 13—10 9 8 7 6 5 4 3 2 1

MANUFACTURED IN THE UNITED STATES OF AMERICA

OVERVIEW OF THE JOURNEY

PREFACE

This book is the result of many people crossing my path over the years. Each one has contributed a bit of this and a bit of that, without which I would never have written this book. The subject is out of character for me, but so needed at this period of time. We live in a time when God doesn't need any more caretakers of the institution. God needs called and equipped leaders who can bring the kingdom to bear on this earth. To them this book is dedicated.

CREDITS

I am especially indebted to Linnea Nilsen Capshaw, who provided a much needed chapter on discovering the call from God, and to Jeff Patton who carefully critiqued the manuscript and offered valuable assistance.

Much of the material comes from personal conversations and e-mails over the past decade. I have not included names for privacy reasons.

Others friends and colleagues have contributed by reading the original manuscript and offering suggestions: Bruce Cole, Robin Trebilcock, Trey Roberson, and Katherine Brearly. I am indebted to them for their kindness and insights.

May all of us hear our call from God and respond with all the strength we can muster.

Bill Easum
Port Aransas, Texas

SECTION 1
A FOUNDATION

A Challenge to *All* Christians

Being Frazzled Wasn't One of
Jesus' Strong Points

Convergence Factors

CHAPTER ONE

A CHALLENGE TO *ALL* CHRISTIANS

This book is addressed to all Christians. The following two stories demonstrate why.

Not Like My Father, Please!

A woman sat across from me, next to her husband, whom we were interviewing for a church planting position. Her comments that day sent chills up my spine.

"Whatever my husband decides will be fine with me as long he doesn't wind up like my father, who was a pastor for forty years. The last half of his ministry turned him into a bitter, spent man. Somewhere along the way the demands of self-centered congregations robbed him of his dreams and he lost sight of his call. I want my husband to do whatever will allow him to retire with the same zeal and love for his call that he has now."

I Never Met a Pastor Who Needed Help

In one of my early church consultations, I was interviewing the chair of a major committee. We were discussing ways to reverse the decline of his church. I said to him,

"You know, one of the issues here is that everyone relies too much on the pastor to do all the ministry."

Before I could finish the man blurted out, "I'm aware our pastor needs help, but we can't afford to hire any more staff."

I couldn't let that one go unanswered, so I responded, "I've never met a pastor who needed help. You don't need more staff. All you need to do is equip your congregation to do ministry."

For a brief moment the man looked at me dumbfounded and perplexed. Then with a hint of sadness in his voice he uttered the most despicable statement a Christian can make: "But we're just laypeople. We're not called to the ministry and we certainly aren't professionals."

If your heart burns within you and you know there must be more to the Christian life than managing conflict, sitting in a pew, serving on a committee, tending to or worshiping with the inmates in the asylum, or praying for early retirement, this book is for you.

The Power of Something Worth Dying For

In 1981, I plunged into one of the darkest periods of my life. The mission from God that I felt was worth dying for was not happening anymore. We were at a standstill. No matter how many staff we added, individuals were not growing and neither was the church. My soul was crushed and I plunged into what Annie Dillard calls the "deeps" where we meet our own personal demons.[1] I would soon learn that the same mission that drove me to despair would also save my soul. Here's my story; it sets the stage for what will follow. Perhaps it is your story also.

I sat quietly, drowning in my own tears. Across from me sat my good friend, parishioner, and renowned surgeon. I had come to his office because I had no other place to turn. I was breaking down. Reality and illusion were running together. It was my wife who suggested I talk with David. I trusted him. We had a bond that dated back to a time I had helped him keep his family together. All I knew was that he would not judge me—he too had been to his "deeps" before.

After a while, he suggested I check into a hospital and get a complete physical to make sure my problem wasn't physical. He was being kind. We both knew my problem was in my soul. But to be sure, I checked in and went through the drill. The diagnosis: I needed to get my act together.

I called together a group of trusted leaders of the church and told them I was resigning as their pastor. To my surprise, they wouldn't accept my resignation. Instead they suggested that I take the next three months off to sort things out. I took their advice, and my wife and our two dogs set out for our beach house.

Over the next three months, I took a journey into hell. The more I examined my vision and where I was with it personally, the more depressed I became. The deeper I went into what some call the "inner journey," the more I realized the impossibility of what I felt God had called me to do. Perhaps I had led the church into an impossible mission.

The vision under which the church and I had been ministering the past eleven years was "Every person is a minister of the gospel of Jesus Christ." We thought it was God's vision for our church. We thought it was a mission worth dying for. But it wasn't happening and we didn't know why. I soon discovered that I was the reason. As long as I kept doing ministries, people would rely on me to do the ministry on their behalf. That realization was intolerable to me and immoral to the God that I worshiped.

What would it take for the mission to go forward? The answer seemed clear. We needed a pastor for every ten to fifteen people. I arrived at this conclusion from observing where most personal conversions and life-changing experiences had happened in my ministry: small groups of ten to fifteen people.

15

However, there was no way we could afford a pastor for every ten to fifteen people. We would need forty to forty-five pastors. Perhaps we could find enough retired pastors? No chance. Besides, they would probably want to do ministry instead of equipping laity for ministry. My depression deepened.

What if we didn't have to pay these pastors? Ever seen a pastor work for nothing? My depression deepened again. Then it dawned on me: what if we trained laypeople to function as unpaid pastors? We had talked about unpaid leaders for years, but no one had applied that concept to the pastors.

I was now at the deepest point of my journey inward. Could laypeople really be trusted with the most sacred of all things: "the" ministry? If they really could be trusted, and if they were adequately equipped, they wouldn't need me anymore. Could I live with that? Now I was at the heart of why we were not achieving our mission. I needed the laity to need me. I was codependent on their need of me. I enjoyed being at the center of attention. I was the one robbing the laity of the joy of ministering to one another in the name of Jesus. The very thought made me sick to my stomach. I was a fraud. My depression deepened.

It was time to fish or cut bait. Either I had to give up my need to be needed or I had to give up the vision, my very reason for living. The latter was not an acceptable option. It was time to grow up and give up control. It was time to live out Ephesians 4:11-12. For the first time in my life, I knew God's solution to my dilemma: equip laypeople to be the pastors of the church. It seemed so simple.

I returned home at the end of the three-month sabbatical to share God's revelation with the leadership. I told them I knew how to remain as their pastor. All we had to do was to provide a pastor for every ten to fifteen people. They were less than impressed with the success of my sabbatical. They looked at me like I was from another planet. Then I walked them through the same steps I had taken in my journey, from paid pastors to unpaid lay pastors. And they understood. Before the end of the evening, two leaders volunteered to be the first lay pastors.

This was not the first time God's vision had both plunged me into the "deeps" and rescued my soul from my own personal hell. During my first year of work on my doctorate, I tried to run away from my call by dropping out of seminary and entering law school. It wasn't long before I was more miserable than ever. Out of the blue, I received a call from the pastor of the church I was attending (in a totally different denomination than the one in which I had started out). He wanted to know if I still wanted to be a minister. I said yes. He said, "You will need to get one course from a United Methodist Seminary, and you can be a minister."

A week later I was sitting in the dean's office at Perkins School of Theology. After some discussion, he said he would not admit me because I had dropped out of seminary once before. I was too big a risk. It was a long ride home from Dallas to Austin, Texas.

I returned home resigned to be a lawyer or a golfer. Again the pastor called and asked me if I really wanted to be a minister. Again, I said yes. Again he said, "Go visit the seminary dean and state your case more forcefully this time." Later I would learn that this pastor and the seminary dean were related.

I returned for a second interview. This time the dean allowed me to audit the courses, but would not allow me to register as a student. In addition, the dean made me spend an hour a week with him to make sure I understood the doctrinal differences between the denomination I was leaving and the one I would be entering. This was my first experience with this kind of denominational nonsense.

I spent two semesters not only taking the one required polity course, but also all of the courses required for a postgraduate degree and passed them all. I had even passed my orals and still I had not been admitted as a full student. My orals committee was shocked when I told them I was just auditing the course in the hope of being admitted as a student.

I learned later that one of the professors giving me my orals went to the dean and demanded to know why I was just auditing the courses. Two days before graduation I called my parents to tell them I had been admitted as a full student and would be graduating in two days. This was not my first experience with God finding a way through whatever obstacle came my way. There have been several other times when such a realization has spurred me on.

My experiences with the "deeps" have taught me much about myself and how God works. What really separates authentic leaders who soar from those who do not is a vision or mission worth dying for. Those who have this kind of vision or mission are able to go on in the face of impossible odds. They are able to focus on the goal so fully that it must happen.

My "deeps" have taught me that my little successes in life have little to do with me and a lot to do with the gracious gift of a mission from God. The mission is what saves us and drives us on—not our ability. The mission is what both drives us down and brings us up. People with a vision don't burn out, they just keep on going and going and going in spite of it all.

A Flawed Beginning

Most books I've read on ministry and leadership are based on three assumptions that lead to flawed conclusions: They make a distinction between the call to professional ministry and the call to lay ministry; they set their conversations about ministry mainly within the context of the institutional church; and they interpret ministry through the eyes of modern thought, ignoring the first few centuries of Christianity. Starting from these perspectives totally flaws any conversation about authentic ministry.

As a result, many Christians are held back from being the kind of person or leader they were created to be, unaware that God has called them to some form of ministry. Too many Christians, both lay and clergy, are following what I describe as "misdirected calls," that is, they have misread their call or have been influenced to abandon their call (see more about misdirected calls in chapters 3 and 5).

Most views on ministry are flawed from the beginning.

This discussion on ministry and leadership will be different because it is mainly based on observations drawn from the New Testament accounts of the early church:

- The call from God is the foundation for all Christian ministry. Jesus demonstrated the call when he chose the disciples. Paul continued the emphasis when he continually referred to himself as called or chosen of God (Romans 1:1 is an example). The call always comes within the context of God's movement in history and is never meant to be confined to the actions of an institution, although it can be affirmed by other leaders (as in Acts 9:28). It is not something that is based on ordination, but is a call from God to all Christians.
- All Christians are called to some form of ministry (1 Peter 2:9-10). The early church understood baptism to be the commissioning service for the ministry of all God's people. The distinctions made between clergy and laity are invalid. Nowhere in the New Testament is any form of *cleros* used to designate a separate class of "ordained" leaders. Instead, it refers to the "inheritance" (from the Greek *clerou*) laid up for all the saints (Colossians 1:12; Acts 2:18). The Greek word *laikos*, which means "laity," is not found in the New Testament. All in the Body of Christ, whether

"saints, bishops, or deacons" (Philemon 1:1), are the "people" of God. "People of God" is a title of honor bestowed upon all who believe in the Lord Jesus Christ (2 Corinthians 10:16; Titus 2:14; 1 Peter 2:9-10). Only one order exists; the *laos*, which means "the people of God." It was not until the third century that the concept of the "laity" was invented by Clement of Alexandria.[2] This error has led to widespread spiritual impotency in the Body of Christ because it has ultimately caused many groups to function in a caste system of clergy and laity. For that reason I will avoid using these terms. Instead, I'll use the terms "pastors" and "Christians" or "Christian leaders."

- The importance of the call to ministry is the same for everyone and all gifts are important to the overall health of the Body (1 Corinthians 12).

- Continuity of faithful witness to the ministry of Jesus Christ was the main concern of the early church rather than continuity of ecclesiastical structure or hierarchy (2 Timothy 2:2). This means two things: one, the life of Jesus is our best example of authentic ministry; and two, ordination is a *call* from God based more on demonstrated faith rather than on a decision made in some top-down hierarchical fashion. Who the leader is and what they do with their life is far more important than any form of academic credentialing or ecclesiastical confirmation.

- Demonstrated credentials were the bases for acknowledging one's leadership role, and the early church gave great latitude in how it understood leadership (Acts 6:3). The early church reacted to spiritual gifts spontaneously and was able to adapt to new forms of leadership to serve the movement (Acts 6:1-7). That's why there is such divergence of thought today on the proper form of leadership. Nothing was as neat then as we have made it today.

- All pastors are called to equip God's people for ministry instead of doing ministry themselves (Ephesians 4:11-12). The ministry of "pastor" is authentic but not in the way we use it today. It does not mean one has been ordained or formally trained. It simply means one has been called by God to equip the Body of Christ for ministry.

These observations lead to the following conclusion:(the key to authentic and effective Christian leadership and living is not found in what we do as much as who we've been called to be and what we are on the inside. Christians have to be true to their call!)

Here, then, is the heart of this book: *You can't give what you don't have!* It is imperative that we keep close to our call, close to our God-given mission, and close to our God. In other words, leaders must take care of themselves and set their own agenda before they can be or do anything for anyone else. I will revisit this theme many times.

It's Not About Us: It's the Mission

A good friend loves to remind people("It's not about me; it's not about you; it's about the mission.")What a change it would make in Christian ministry if you and I took this simple statement to heart. Ministry wouldn't be about what we want or need, it would be about what God has prepared us to be.

I'm convinced that the majority of Christians today, lay and clergy, are not involved in the kind of ministry for which God created them. Either they have drifted away from their original call, or they are unaware that God has called them to some form of ministry.

Many Christians are going through life totally unaware that God is calling them to some form of ministry. Sitting in a pew or on a committee is certainly not the essence of ministry. *To not know one has been called to some form of ministry or to not respond to God's call is to die without ever really living!* If this last statement describes you, welcome relief will be offered later in the book.

I'm equally convinced that many pastors are unhappily going through the motions of ministry. Somewhere along the way many have given up on living out their call. Some are confused about why they signed on for one type of ministry and now the churches they serve force them to do another kind. Some are bitter because of the congregational environments in which they find themselves. Others are so demoralized or angry they are looking forward to retirement and they haven't even reached fifty. Based on my interaction with thousands of pastors, my guess is that 30 percent of them would do something else with their life if they thought they could make a decent living.[3]

If you desire in your heart to be more effective in your ministry, this book is for you. It will assist you in rediscovering or reaffirming a God-directed ministry for your life and that of your congregation.

Three Blips on My Radar Screen

Three kinds of Christians are appearing as blips on my radar screen as I travel around.

All three of these blips appear desperately in need of spiritual renewal. The first is totally demoralized; the second is very close to falling off the edge; and the third is simply drifting through life not knowing he or she isn't contributing much to the kingdom.

More and more pastors are leaving ministry or retiring early. For some, the times in which we live seem to be changing too much and too fast for them to keep up. For others, the adrenalin of success appears to drive them closer and closer to the edge. Others are just adrift. All are in need of renewal.

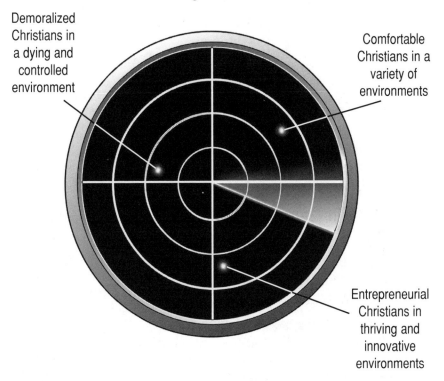

Demoralized Christians in a dying and controlled environment

Comfortable Christians in a variety of environments

Entrepreneurial Christians in thriving and innovative environments

More and more laity are asking the question, "Isn't there more to Christianity than this?" Perhaps you've asked this question. You know deep down that Christ died for more than you are experiencing in your Christian walk.

If you fall into one of these three categories, you need to remember that you're not alone. Jesus had such times. However, he knew how to handle life. On more than one occasion when he had reached his personal limit, he pulled away from the crowds, sometimes leaving them in desperate situations. Often he wasn't even nice about it. Jesus knew when to withdraw and renew himself. Everyone, sooner or later, needs to acknowledge the need for spiritual renewal and withdraw, even if it means leaving some people in a mess for a while.

The Reason for This Book

The conclusions I've shared in this chapter sadden me. But I've worked as a consultant with too many church leaders to reach any other conclusions. They also caused me to write this book.

> **God calls ALL Christians to some form of service. To miss that call is to live without living.**

I'm not known as a touchy-feely guy. I never dreamed I would write this kind of book. It's different from anything I have ever written before. But the mission demands it. It's not about me or what I prefer writing about, it's about the mission. *Too many of God's people are living and dying without ever really living.* God calls each of us to something better. In fact, God calls us to tackle the world and change it. That kind of mission demands healthy, God-directed Christians. It's time to clean out the cobwebs, discard our fears, and awaken from our spiritual comas.

This book will encourage us all to do one of the following:

- Rediscover that primal, naïve, original moment with God that left us feeling as if we could change the world.
- Discover for the first time the indescribable experience of feeling called by God to serve the mission.

My prayer for you is that as you read this book and work through the exercises, a refining fire will be kindled in your inner being that will infect everyone you meet. If we can reclaim or discover that primal moment with God, and let it direct our lives and our ministry, the world will be different from us being in it.

How to Use This Book

This book is designed to allow you to choose the material that might be most helpful to you. Of course, it is best if you read the entire book since you may never know where God is lurking. However, you will have choices to make along the way. Make them based on where you are on your spiritual journey.

Here's how it works. Each chapter contains basic information everyone needs to incarnate within himself or herself in order to be an authentic and effective Christian. At various points, I will alert you to an appendix that applies to the spiritual issue being addressed. If that issue speaks to your present situation and you want to read more on the subject, then read that appendix.

REFLECTION TIME

Begin a journal. As you read and do the exercises, record your thoughts, feelings, observations, and fitting Scripture texts. From time to time, revisit your comments and see if anything is changing or if you seem stuck in a rut. At the end of the book you will be asked to review your notes for a very special personal project.

A form for the journal is supplied in appendix 1.

Notes

1. Annie Dillard, *Teaching a Stone to Talk* (New York: Harper & Row, 1982), pp. 94-95.

2. Alexandre Faivre, *The Emergence of the Laity in the Early Church*, trans. David Smith (New York: Paulist Press, 1990).

3. This estimate is based on the mental notes I have made over the past fifteen years as a consultant to churches and pastors.

CHAPTER TWO

BEING FRAZZLED WASN'T ONE OF JESUS' STRONG POINTS

Every time I fly on a commercial plane I have to listen to this dumb statement: "Before helping someone else with their oxygen mask, put yours on first." I usually tune this announcement out. But one day, I didn't. Instead, I found myself running through my head the reasons why airline personnel are so paranoid about us putting on our own oxygen mask first. Surely if the person sitting beside me couldn't get his or her mask on and appeared in trouble, I should put his or hers on first. But the more I thought about it the more I realized they had a point. To not put mine on first could be a fatal mistake. You see, if the person next to me needed my help putting the mask on, something else was wrong with him or her. He or she was too weak or confused or hurt to put it on and, even if I got his or hers on, more than likely the person would not be able to help me put mine on and I would probably pass out before putting on my own mask. Whereas, if I quickly put mine on, the odds are I would be able to get his or hers on in time since I was strong enough to help myself in the first place.

Now, what do oxygen masks have to do with rediscovering ministry? Everything! Too many Christians are so busy they don't take time to develop their spiritual life. They

27

remind me of the hamster on the treadmill—constantly running to nowhere, refusing to get off the treadmill long enough to spend time developing their inner life. Too many Christians I know look like they just stuck their finger in a light socket. What most of us need to do is get off the treadmill, pull our finger out of the socket, and put on our own oxygen mask before we go into a spiritual coma and die.

Remember—you can't give what you don't have. If you hope to develop spiritual giants, you must be a spiritual giant. If your dream is to develop a group of committed disciples who will turn the world upside down, your commitment must be off the charts. If you want courageous Christians who will venture out on faith and risk it all, you must have the kind of courage that inspires others to be willing to risk it all. You can't give what you don't have.

A lack of spiritual oxygen is the primary reason so many of our churches function more like hospices and funeral homes than the church we see in the New Testament. This deprivation of spiritual oxygen is why more and more Christians are falling victim to various forms of addiction. This lack of spiritual oxygen explains why so many pastors are reaching the end of their ministry burned out and bitter and why so many Christians have little more to show for their faith than a backside that is contoured to the church pews and a brain fried from too many meetings.)

How rich is your spiritual oxygen?

No organization, not even a church, ever has more vitality than those who lead it. If the leaders are starving for spiritual oxygen, then so are those they lead. The problem today with most segments of established Christianity is that our leaders are stunted spiritually. It's time for Christians to put on their oxygen masks and to breathe into their lives the living presence of an awesome God. By doing so, they just might rediscover authentic and effective ministry.

When the spiritual oxygen is rich and our relationship with Christ is growing daily, Christians are keenly aware of the following eternal truths about leadership:

- Leaders need leaders who are spiritually ahead of them. This type of leadership takes constant devotion and learning.
- Leaders set the tone for a congregation. If the congregation is weak, the leaders are weak.
- In the absence of strong leadership, leaders leave and dysfunctional people take charge.
- Leaders always take responsibility for whatever situation in which they find themselves. Leaders never blame the system for their failure. If the system destroys them, they allowed it to happen.
- Leaders set their own agenda and set out on the journey to make it happen. It is silly to think that a pastor should do whatever a congregation wants him or her to do. That would be a violation of a pastor's

call. The same is true for all Christians. It is a violation of God's direction for our lives to allow someone else to redirect our call.

• Leaders get what they look for.

Jesus Shows Us the Way

The life and teachings of Jesus, as they are recorded by the early church, are the basis for understanding authentic and effective leadership and ministry in any age. His basic legacy was a team of eleven (he lost one) transformed and uneducated disciples who would, along with a few other people, such as Paul, change everything forever. He spent the bulk of his time doing two things with his disciples—modeling faith and equipping them to be the leaders of tomorrow.

Jesus saw the role of leadership to be that of radically transforming the hearts and minds of people. Two classic texts explain his view of the essence of ministry—Matthew 28:18-19 and John 21:16.

The First and Second Great Commissions

The last words the early church recorded Jesus saying have to do with making disciples of all the people groups in the world. "All authority in heaven and on earth has been given to me. Go therefore and make disciples of all nations, baptizing them in the name of the Father and of the Son and of the Holy Spirit, and teaching them to obey everything that I have commanded you. And remember, I am with you always, to the end of the age" (Matthew 28:18-20).

We are challenged to make disciples because all authority has been given to Jesus by God. Jesus' command is an imperative, leaving no room for equivocation on our part. We have no choice but to "go" and disciple the world. To ignore this commission is to ignore Christ!

The same theme is recorded in Acts 1:8 by the early church at the last appearance of Jesus. "You shall be my witnesses in Jerusalem, in all Judea and Samaria, and to the ends of the earth." The word "witness" means martyr. We are to totally give ourselves to take the good news to the streets! However, it is not enough just to disciple people. Jesus gives us another imperative—we are to care for God's people. "A second time [Jesus] said to him, 'Simon son of John, do you love me?' He said to him, 'Yes, Lord; you know that I love you.' Jesus said to him, 'Tend my sheep' " (John 21:16). Some texts say "feed my sheep."

The problem with this text is that most of us read it without any knowledge of the role of a shepherd in Jesus' day. Shepherds didn't feed sheep. Instead, they had two basic functions. The first was to make sure that the sheep had pastures with enough grass to eat. And second, they were to keep them safe from any predators. The key to understanding Jesus' statement to Peter is to ask why did shepherds tend sheep in the first place. It certainly wasn't because they smelled good. No, the reason they tended sheep and made sure they had a safe place to graze was because they wanted them to grow and reproduce to make more sheep. Sheep, not the shepherd, begat sheep. Thus, what Jesus said to Peter was make sure my people are so nurtured that they are able to make disciples. Your role, Peter, is to equip them to be disciple-makers.

> To care for one another and to make disciples is the heart of Christianity.

Taken together, these two texts sum up the primary ministry and mission of God's people—we are to care for and transform people.

But here's the rub. Transforming people requires that you love them, care for them, and equip them after they have been transformed. However, too many pastors take care of people without ever transforming anyone and a lot of Christians are happy to simply be cared for without any thought for those around them who do not know Christ. Pastors spend the bulk of their time visiting hospitals and shut-ins, doing the priesthood of all believers, going to meetings, writing sermons, counseling, arbitrating church fights, and at best trying to get a few souls to follow their lead. Such action is not what Jesus intended. Christians are called by our Lord to care for the church *and* to make disciples of the world. To be the church, Christians must be responsible for both.

Making disciples who do God's will is the bedrock passion of authentic Christianity. Pastors are called to equip God's people. And God's people are called to transform the world. Somewhere along the way, too many of us have lost this passion. In its place we put a desire to care for others and help them achieve whatever it is that they desire to do with their life and church. Like Aaron, we help them build a golden calf.

Jesus was a transformer who cared for people enough to do more than just care for them—he transformed them into people who sought God's will and helped others do the same. In John 13:15, Jesus said, "I have set you an example, that you also should do as I have done for you."

The journey from caregiver to transformer is the most important issue facing Christianity today. Unless more of us take this journey, most of our established churches will continue to decline. Worse than that, people will continue to live and die without a clue of what God is doing in the world and what God wants them to do with their life. Such a tragedy must not be allowed to continue.

Jesus Put On His Own Oxygen Mask First

Becoming a transformational Christian will not be easy for some. We have been trained and conditioned to function as caregivers with a maintenance orientation for a defined group or a building, rather than transformers who change hearts, lives, and cities. Responding to this call will require most of us to retool from being Christians who care for the flock, to transformers of hearts and minds.

Jesus knew it wouldn't be easy to be this kind of leader so he spent a lot of time on his own spirituality. He knew the principle that you can't give what you don't have. In John 17, the early church records how Jesus prepared himself to be able to help us all become transformers in our own way.

> **Jesus took care of himself first. Do you?**

The first time I read the Bible I was sixteen and a half years old. One of the things that struck me most in my first reading was that Jesus was on vacation a lot of the time! (Non-Christians and new Christians often see things that longtime Christians don't.) On several occasions, Jesus demonstrated his need to put on his own oxygen mask first by withdrawing from his friends. He knew that he couldn't give what he didn't have. So all throughout his life when he ran short, he would withdraw to renew himself. Whenever he felt drained, he would get lost from the crowd. At times, he would even abandon the Twelve in order to be alone with God. Jesus put on his own oxygen mask first. He took care of himself. He had to if he was going to give us what we needed.

You've probably read or heard John 17 sometime in your life. It's just one of those gems that can't be ignored. Jesus is in the last hours of his life. Obviously he is nervous about his future date with death. Who wouldn't be? So he withdraws to pray and care for his aching soul.

Jesus begins his prayer by putting on his own oxygen mask first—he prays for himself and asks God to glorify him that he might have strength. He didn't pray for others or for the world, he prayed for himself. He knew that he couldn't give what he didn't have. He knew that in troubled times, like those awaiting him, his only hope was in his growing relationship with God. Only God would do at this point in his ministry.

Do you pray for yourself before praying for anyone else? If asking you to pray for yourself at first seems selfish to you, then you haven't gotten the concept yet—you can't give what you don't have. If you want to be an authentic and effective Christian, you must care for yourself before you care for others.

You must nurture your relationship with God, just like Jesus did. Leadership is about modeling a deep spiritual connection with God so that others are inspired to grow their own relations. This spiritual depth is the only source of authenticity and authority a Christian has in this emerging world. If you need examples of withdrawal opportunities, turn to appendix 2.

We live in a very troubled period of time in the world. Wars and terrorism are rampant. However, the most serious war and terrorism happening today is spiritual. As Christendom[1] comes to a close, and with it all of the rules by which the game of life has been played for sixteen centuries, Christians are finding themselves in a strange new world—a pagan culture in which Christianity is no longer the established religion. Everywhere we turn congregations are struggling to survive and Christians no longer seem to have a story worth telling. In such times it has always been true that the way forward for God's people has been through personal renewal. Throughout history, God's people have survived and thrived only through nurturing their relationship with God.

The same is true when one is struggling with one's own personal demons. We must first nurture our relationship with God because we are no help to others unless we are strong in our faith.

It was only after he prayed for himself that Jesus prayed for his disciples and finally for those who would believe due to the ministry of his disciples. Jesus never prayed for the world; he only prayed for those who would carry and respond to the message. For whom are you praying?

The Next Step in the Journey

People with a vision don't burn out, give up, or compromise. They carry on, no matter what. The key to spiritual leadership is to withdraw, not to work harder. The key is to allow enough time in the day to nurture your soul so that you have something earth-shattering to share with others.

REFLECTION TIME

- How much time do you spend putting on your own oxygen mask? Is it enough? If not, what do you need to rearrange in your life to find the time?
- When was the last time you prayed for yourself? How did it feel?
- How do you feel about setting your agenda for ministry rather than allowing the congregation to set it? Does that make you feel dictatorial or selfish? Why?
- Make a list in your journal of those things that seem to be keeping you from hearing and responding to God's call. Pray about them and ask God what you should do about them.
- Remember that appendix 2, "Opportunities for Withdrawal," was mentioned in this chapter.

Note

1. Christendom refers to the last sixteen hundred years since Constantine made Christianity the favored, and eventually the established, religion of the Roman Empire.

CHAPTER THREE

CONVERGENCE FACTORS

My work with church leaders has taught me that four factors usually converge to make an authentic and effective leader: a call from God, preferred leadership style, the context in which leaders find themselves, and his or her skill set. I call these the "Convergence Factors."

Call + Style + Context + Skill Set = Authentic and Effective Leadership

The key to self-fulfillment as a leader is to understand the convergence of all four of these issues. Many Christians want to make a difference in their church, but no matter how hard they try, they aren't effective. Consider this e-mail I received while writing this chapter.

Subject: **Stuck**
Date: 5/26/2003 12:10 AM Central Standard Time
From: Youknowwho.com
To: Easum

Hi, Bill.
    I attended the Turnaround Pastor seminar last October and came away with hopes and dreams of

turning around the church I serve. I came away with increased hopes and dreams of moving the church forward. This does not seem to be happening. I try to apply what I have learned, but oftentimes find myself frustrated because there just does not seem to be the interest in the congregation.

Today I am discouraged, not knowing where to turn, not knowing if it is me or the nature of the church or what. I can't seem to inspire follow-through or find enough "eyes that light up" at the vision. There are a goodly number of folks who love the church, message, services, and me as their minister, but don't seem to have a hunger for outreach or the fulfillment of the church mission that they together created.

I am questioning whether I am simply spinning my wheels wanting more. While I do try to do the things I learned, I find it often a struggle. I was a success in the secular world as a sales manager with a large sales force, and with a passion to serve God I truly believed that I could grow a vibrant, exciting, transformative church.

I was reading an article on small church dynamics, and was concerned about a couple of things I read that lead me to question whether or not I have what it takes to lead a small church, such as a relational style.

Does "leadership style" really matter? Can or should one change their style to remain in the church they are serving? How can I tell if I am the problem?

Thanks for listening.

It would seem that success in sales in the secular world would have prepared this person for success in ministry, but not so in this case. This person desperately wants to make a difference in the church, but doesn't seem able to do so. Perhaps the call is misdirected, or worse yet, nonexistent. Maybe the preferred leadership style is conflicting with the person's hopes and dreams. Maybe the context in which this person is serving is too dysfunctional to be much more than it is. Or perhaps this person just doesn't have the skill set to be a leader. What makes the situation even worse, no one but this person can decipher the truth. Christians can go to conference after conference, read all the books, pray without ceasing, and still their hearts break because they can't achieve their hopes and dreams.

I've worked with hundreds of Christians who have voiced similar longings about their ministry. They yearn to be more effective and authentic in how they serve their Christ. Yet they don't seem to be able to reach their potential. It's because one or more of the Convergence Factors are incompatible with the person.

Convergence Factors

- Call
- Preferred leadership style
- Context of ministry
- Skill set

What's a Person to Do?

I know it sounds simple, but we must realize the importance played by all four of these factors. For a leader to reach his or her potential, all four of these factors must be compatible. If they aren't, a person has two choices: either to learn to live with the consequences of being ineffective or frustrated, or do whatever is necessary to change the incompatible factors.

Unfortunately, I see many Christians doing neither. They continue to build up their hopes and dreams for making a difference without making the necessary changes. As a result, their frustration level reaches unbearable proportions and they are doomed to a life of frustration and despair.

Let's Begin the Journey

Wherever you find yourself in this scenario, my goal is to assist you on your journey to authentic and effective ministry. Most of this book is focused on two Convergence Factors—the call and the preferred style of leadership. These two, more than any of the other Convergence Factors, shape the heart of a leader. I will, however, examine the role played by context and skill set. So, let's begin.

CHAPTER FOUR

THE EXPERIENCE THAT CHANGES EVERYTHING

Hearing and answering a call from God is the most awesome, life-changing moment a human being ever experiences. No one is the same ever again. Not only is the person changed, but also the way that person goes about exercising his or her faith undergoes radical transformation. Let's look at what this means.

What Is a Call?

The call is that moment when Christians find out why God put them on this planet. It defines our life and ministry. To go through life without ever experiencing and responding to this call is to die without ever having lived.

Many different kinds of calls exist.

The call is a foundational experience in the life of God's people in both the Old and New Testaments. Some calls were dramatic, some not so dramatic. Some calls were very specific and some were more generic in nature. Some calls were to full-time commitment and some were to be lived out in some other vocation. Other calls are more like a burr under

43

the saddle than a glorious experience. But all calls leave the person with a different view on how to spend his or her life for God.

Whether the call is a burning bush, a big fish, a meditative moment, or a blinding light, a call not only changes a life, it also precedes all effective, authentic ministry. By "ministry" I mean much more than putting on church programs or sitting on a board, or being a faithful member of a committee. Authentic ministry goes beyond these institutional trappings. Authentic ministry is always first an idea born in the heart of God. Authentic ministry always leads to some form of service to others in the name of Jesus Christ. That kind of ministry can begin in a meeting but can never be contained or achieved in a meeting or even a program.

In an earlier book, *Leadership on the OtherSide,* I wrote that the foundation of all leadership is a radical obedience to a call bigger than one's own life. What I've learned over the years is that the more specific the call is, the larger-than-life the call becomes.

Is your call big enough to die for?

This foundation involves two things: obedience and call. Any form of authentic Christian living, much less ministry, requires both. Without obedience to what God wants accomplished through our lives, we can't fulfill our call and reach our God-given potential. Therefore a call is not a job or a task laid on us. It's not some personal vendetta or cause that we choose to follow. It's not the result of some nomination and election process. A call is the way God expresses to us why we were put on this planet. Without hearing and obeying God's call, we simply go about doing whatever someone else asks us to do on behalf of the church. Such action is not the essence of authentic ministry.

Because of their call, Christians do what has to be done to achieve God's mission for their life. Being obedient to this mission is an all-consuming passion for their life.

And because our obedience to our call is so all-consuming, we are able to be flexible on most other things, such as style and methods. The result of our obedience to this call is a deep, burning passion to carry out the mission God has given. Whatever allows that mission to flourish is all that matters. For this reason, people following a call don't get caught up in wrangling over details such as style and method. Instead, they just ask one thing—if I do this, will it help me carry out my calling? This simple question was the driving force behind Paul's preaching on Mars Hill to the unknown God. It was also why he could say, "I have become all things to all people, that I might by all possible means save some" (1 Corinthians 9:22). Think of how that understanding of calling and mission would change the way your church does ministry.

The Power of Your Call

Whenever I'm in trouble or lose my sense of direction, I find myself revisiting my call to preach. Doing so has never failed to lift my spirits, refocus my direction, and relight my passion for ministry. It can do the same for you. I've heard hundreds of testimonies to the power of the call to both direct and redirect someone's life and ministry.

The following e-mail from Sally and my response shows how all-consuming your call should be in your life.

Subject: **Questions**
Date: 4/21/2003 11:00:53 AM Central Standard Time
From: Sa@timbuktoo.com
To: Easum

Dear Bill,
 When we were meeting last year, a couple of very practical questions came up that I would like to get

your input on when you have the opportunity. What are the things you look for as you look at a new congregation to see if they are able and willing to be in a "transformational" mold? I didn't see that as I came to my present congregation and would like to be able to spot a little better when a congregation wants a "chaplain" and when they want to move on to a more vibrant, alive future.

What are the first things that you set up as soon as you would get to a new congregation that help get a quick start on the process of moving folks toward ministry and away from entitlement? In my present call, I was dumbfounded that there was no focus, no process for renewing—moving forward—here when I got here. It has taken me a long time to figure out any steps to move the congregation forward.

Sally

Questions like those posed in Sally's e-mail aren't easy questions to answer since the context of each new pastorate can be so different. But these questions come up too often to pass them off as impossible to answer. So, here is how I responded to Sally.

Subject: **Re:Questions**	
Date:	4/21/2003 12:10 AM Central Standard Time
From:	Easum@aol.com
To:	Sa@timbuktoo.com

First of all, Sally, never take at face value what a search committee tells you. Many times they don't have a clue about what they want. Other times they think they know what they want until faced with the implications. I remember one consultation where the church told me they wanted to reach more young people when what they really meant was they wanted to reach more young people who acted like old people.

So, Sally, you must dig much deeper to find out what they really mean. Sure, they will tell you they want to grow. What they don't tell you is that they want to grow as long as it is on their terms and doesn't cause any pain. So get very specific with them about who you are and what God has called you to do. I guarantee you if you don't know what you're about, the congregation will quickly tell you. So, set your own agenda.

You see, Sally, the real issue is not so much are they in a transformational mode, as are you? You have a call from God. Follow it. You must never fit your call into their agenda. If what God has called you to do doesn't match what they want to happen, don't do what they want! Nothing good can come of it. So get very specific with them about what God has called you to do.

Keep in mind that the more specific your call is the more effective you will be as a leader. If your call isn't specific enough to give serious direction to your choices, you will most likely drift through your ministry doing what others want done rather then following God's claim on your life. It's stupid to assume that you must fit your call into what they want. It should be the other way around. If it doesn't match, then you shouldn't be their pastor.

So my first response, Sally, is "What has God called you to do?" Whatever it is, don't let any congregation derail you in fulfilling that call. When you interview with the search committee share your call with them and make sure they understand that you work for God, not them. Say to them, "Here is the mission that I am on; does it match with your mission?" This is what God has called me to do as a pastor; how does it match up with what you hope to achieve over the next few years?" If they can't handle that, don't accept the call to pastor that church. Surely God wouldn't send you to a place where you weren't expected to follow your call.

Second, Sally, based on your understanding of your call, make a list of responsibilities you feel called to perform and ask the committee to rate them based on what they want from a pastor. Here's the list I would give them if I were interviewing for the position. I have put the responsibilities in the order in which I would hope they would rank them. Of course, you need to make up your own list and rank it according to your calling.

Please mark the following in the order of importance based on what you expect from your pastor.

_____ Modeling spiritual leadership
_____ Mentoring key leaders paid and unpaid into spiritual giants
_____ Equipping key leaders paid and unpaid for hands-on, team-based ministry
_____ Seeing the big picture and communicating it to the congregation
_____ Overseeing the best worship experience in town
_____ Overseeing the care and feeding of the congregation
_____ Raising up new adult leaders
_____ Encouraging the youth to share in the ministry
_____ What's not in the above list that you feel is more important than what's listed?

As you see from the list, Sally, I have led them in the direction my call has taken me. You should do the same. If transformation is your goal, as your e-mail suggests, then the above will work for you. My guess is the list will provide fodder for much conversation. I would be prepared to back up the list with some biblical examples, story or text.

Now, let's assume that you are now the pastor of this congregation. What you do your first year is based on what you are called to do. If you are serious about transformation, then forget most of what you have heard you should do the first year. Usually it's wrong. Whatever you do, don't spend the first year doing nothing but getting to know them. That is a formula for failure. By the time you are ready to take action, the people who hoped you would be a leader have given up on you and the Controllers, if there are any, feel as if they can manipulate you. So, strike while the iron is hot!

Sally, here's what I would do.

I would arrive casting a specific vision and seeing whose eyes lighted up when they heard the vision. I would gather these folks into a small group and mentor them until they were ready to assume major leadership in the church. When the time comes, move them into leadership.

I'd immediately try to bring into the church a number of new people, especially new Christians. That means I would spend more time away from the church than within it. This would probably mean that I would have to miss some regular meetings and that I might have to explain why to the present leaders. Perhaps the parable of the Lost Sheep might help here.

Next, I would preach the entire first year from the great transformational texts, especially from Acts, so that they can see what a church is like and what it does (you will find a list of some of these texts in an article I did in the May 2001 edition of Net Results titled "Nine Texts For Our Time"). I would pick the key transformational moments in the life of church, especially those where the early Christians are caused to reach out into the world, such as Peter going to Cornelius even though he really didn't want to go.

I would gather as many from the congregation as were willing into small home groups to explore their hopes and dreams. My goal here would be to listen so well that I could repeat back to them a synthesized version of those hopes and dreams. My hope would be that their hopes and dreams might provide the foundation from which to launch the new direction.

Finally, if needed, I would try to create a quick victory or two. Most small churches don't believe in themselves much anymore. A quick victory is needed sometimes.

> Sally, all of this needs to be shifted through the lens
> of your call and the context in which you find yourself.
> Above all, stay close to your call and have fun.
> Let me know if this isn't enough.
> Bill

Can you remember your call? Are you as close to it now as when you first experienced it? Can you still feel the tingles that went up your spine as you felt the awe and then the submission? Do you still think of it as a significant turning point in your life? When you're in crises, does revisiting your call cause you to soar once again? Is it specific enough that it gives direction to your life?

A Great Heresy

One of the great heresies experienced by Christianity is the unwritten belief that the call is reserved mostly for clergy. When I was a young man, it was assumed that most people who felt called would enter some form of full-time Christian service. Very few understood that laypeople could be called to serious ministry in their local church. Everyone just understood that "real" ministry belonged to the clergy.

Unfortunately, too many people still believe this heresy. They call on their pastor to pray, hold him or her to higher standards than the general membership, and use their pastor as a spiritual hired gun to carry out *the* ministry of the church. When anyone receives a call to ministry, people just naturally assume that God is calling them into ordained ministry. But nothing could be farther from the truth. God calls every Christian to some form of ministry and ordination has nothing to do with it!

The Bible tells many stories about God calling unlikely and untrained people to do extraordinary things. In fact, many of the people God called were less than admirable people—David, Paul, and Zaccheus, to mention a few. None of the disciples had any formal training. We're reminded in 1 Peter 2:9 that all of God's people "are a chosen race, a royal priesthood." I don't often quote from another source, but in this case I'll make an exception. In their book, *Calling,* Frank Tillapaugh and Richard Hurst remind us that "Every time we refer to vocational clergy as 'the minister,' we drive nails into the coffin of the priesthood of the believer."[1]

Never have a doubt about it; God calls every Christian to some form of service. But if you still have doubts, read Ephesians 4:11-12, "It was he who gave some to be apostles, some to be prophets, some to be evangelists, and some to be pastors and teachers, to prepare God's people for works of service, so that the body of Christ may be built up" (NIV).

This text is crystal clear: the role of a pastor is not to do ministry, nor to take care of people, but to prepare or equip God's people for ministry. God's people, the *laos,* are the primary source of ministry. If that is true, then the call comes to all of God's people. The pastor's primary role is to prepare them to live out that calling. This understanding of God's intent for the church is much different than a group of leaders deciding what program the church should do and then looking to people to make that program happen.

This text boils down to two realities:

• Pastors should set their own agenda of equipping God's people for ministry whether their church wants them to or not.
• God's people should seek God's will for their lives and do whatever is necessary to live out that calling.[2]

Three Tragedies

This heresy has caused three tragedies. First, many Christians act as if they are second-class Christians. Why else would so many Christians say, "But I'm just a layperson"? Listen to the helplessness of this e-mail:

Subject: **We need help**
Date: 10/3/2002 1:04:08 PM Central Standard Time
From: Sharon@dance.com
To: Easum

Our church really needs a strong leader. We've been declining now for as long as I can remember. Pastors come and go and nothing seems to change. None of them seem to have a clue about what to do. Of course, some of our members don't help. It seems that no matter what our pastor suggests, they always find a way to scuttle it. What's funny, that group is only a handful of folks. I try to do what I can, but it always winds up in a fight. It's not nice to fight in church. I know they shouldn't be allowed to lead, but I can't do much about it. I'm just a layperson.

Second, most Christians have thought that if they felt called to ministry they had to be ordained. I received this e-mail from a layperson in a typical mainline church.

Subject: **Called but frustrated**
Date: 06/11/1999 11:19:04 PM Central Standard Time
From: Mike@backdraft.com
To: Easum

I feel called by God to lead in a significant way, but not full-time. And I don't want to preach either. But when I talk with my pastor, I get the feeling that significant ministry requires that I have to go through some kind of indoctrination period and become a pastor. I don't want to be a pastor. I just want to serve

God in a very specific way. I also don't want to be on a staff and I don't want to be paid. When I tell that to my pastor, it's like a blank wall. It's as if my pastor doesn't understand.

Third, it has caused congregations to rely far too much on their pastor. Read this sad e-mail I received some years ago. Please pardon the French.

Subject: **I've had it**
Date: 06/11/1999 11:19:04 PM Central Standard Time
From: JR@maildrop.com
To: Easum

I've had it. Everyone wants a piece of me and I've just had it. I feel like nothing more than a hired gun. It's as if everyone relies on me for everything. I want to serve, but I really don't like kissing a**.

I refer to these tragedies as "misdirected calls." Too many people are simply not following their God-given call. In the next chapter we'll take a further look at what I mean by "misdirected calls."

REFLECTION TIME

- What's wrong with the following comment made by many church leaders? "I was called into *the* ministry."
- Was there a time in your life when your call was clearer and stronger? If so, why are you farther from it now than you were in the past? List the reasons in your journal. If not, is your understanding of your call greater now than when you received it? If so, how? Make a list.
- Is your call worthy of dying for? If not, why? How do you feel about that? Does your calling seem too small? If so, spend some time listening to God and let God expand it. If your call seems too big, spend time sharpening it until it is something you and God can get your arms around. Write your conclusions in your journal. You may need this later when you write your personal mission statement.
- Spend time each day reflecting on this prayer: "Lord put me in the center of your will. Show me what you are doing in this world and let me be a part of it." Pay attention to what you hear God saying to you. Write down anything you hear from

God and share it with your spouse or close friend.
- Read the book *Calling* by Tillapaugh and Hurst.
- Those who love classical music might want to listen to Leonard Bernstein's *Mass*. It is the story of a priest who recovered the joy of his faith. A Web site containing all of Bernstein's work is found at http://memory.loc.gov/ammem/lbhtml/lbhome.html.
- Read 1 Corinthians 1:26-31. Does it raise any anxieties about fulfilling your call? If so, who do you know that you can share them with?

Notes

1. Frank Tillapaugh and Richard Hurst, *Calling* (Monument, Colo.: Dreamtime Publishing, 1997), p. 59.

2. For more on the role of God's people in ministry, see the landmark book, Greg Ogden, *Unfinished Business: Returning the Ministry to the People of God,* rev. ed. (Grand Rapids: Zondervan, 2003).

CHAPTER FIVE

MISDIRECTED CALLS

Often an unspoken uneasiness lurks just beneath the surface of many Christians. No one wants to talk openly about this uneasiness, but they talk to me about it privately, as you will see later. I don't mean any disrespect by what you're about to read. I just think it's time some of us faced reality: *many Christian leaders (clergy and lay) have been duped into following the wrong call and are wasting their own lives and the lives of those under their influence.*

Give me time to explain before you start heating up the tar and ripping up the pillows. For most of the last fifty years, when someone received a call to preach, it mostly meant that God had chosen him or her to become a pastor of a church. To make matters worse, ministry was mostly relegated to the paid clergy. Most calls sent the person to seminary to some form of full-time Christian service. Very few understood that laypeople could be called to serious ministry in their local church. I can still remember saying "I surrendered to *the* ministry" as if there were only one form of ministry. Can you hear those nails being driven?

> Many Christians are following the wrong call!

Not until recently have established congregations begun to understand and practice the belief that all Christians receive a call from God to ministry. This means that there isn't such a thing as *the* ministry. There are ministries galore, open to all Christians. One doesn't have to go into ordained ministry to be in ministry.

If this is an accurate view of what has happened, then there are probably a lot of ordained clergy who were never called to be the pastor of a congregation. Some were called to be apostles, and others were called to ministries such as chaplains and counselors, but not to be pastors of congregations. It also means that there are a lot of Christians who have never heard God's call nor been involved in ministry because they assumed one had to become a pastor to answer *the* call to ministry.

Here are four conversations I've had over the years. Each one represents many other similar conversations.

Misdirected Story #1

Subject: **Do I have to go to seminary?**		
Date:	3/13/2002 6:34:35 PM Pacific Standard Time	
From:	Preacher@surfire.com	
To:	Easum	

I always felt uncomfortable as a pastor. Almost as if I wasn't suppose to be one. I never enjoyed most of the things the congregations expected of me. But it never dawned on me that I might have misunderstood my call. After all, I felt called by God to be involved in ministry and my pastor told me I had to go to seminary if I wanted to pastor a church. How in the world did he and I make the leap from a call to ministry to a call to pastor a church? Isn't there some kind of an in-between? Can't a person be called to ministry and not be a pastor of a church? Why did my pastor direct me to seminary when all I really needed was some coaching in the basics of using the gifts God gave me?

Misdirected Story #2

A couple of years ago I was leading a small group of pastors in developing leadership skills. I had just finished a whole day of work on the role of the pastor, giving special interest to the role of equipping laity to do the work of ministry rather than the pastor doing most of it, such as going to the hospital, visiting shut-ins, and going to meetings. When I finished, a middle-aged man on my right said to me, "If I did what you are recommending, there would be no need for me to be a pastor. I entered *the* ministry because it felt good for people to need me. If I did what you advocate, they wouldn't need me anymore. Then where would I be?" This man had not been called by God to perform the role of pastor as described in Ephesians 4:11-12. He had spent his whole life thinking he was following God's call, when all he had achieved his entire ministry was to keep congregations dependent on him so that he would feel good about himself and find some validation for his life.

Misdirected Story #3

I just finished speaking to a large group of people on the subject of the role of leaders in today's world. Of course, when it came to pastors, I stressed that their only biblical role is to be that of an equipper. I was just about finished putting away my computer and projector when a man approached me. He had tears in his eyes and was visibly shaken. I asked him if I could help him. He replied, "I'm one of those leaders you just talked about. I've been to seminary, pastored churches now for twenty years, and I'm just now discovering that I wasn't called to pastor a church. I shouldn't have gone to seminary. I should have followed my heart and been a veterinarian and used my gift of evangelism as a layperson, but that wasn't acceptable back then. Now, I'm too old to go back to school and I'm not trained to be anything but a theologian, and not a very good one at that. I could have won many more people as a layperson!"

Thousands of pastors are trapped like this forty-five-year-old man—not called to pastor and not trained to do anything else. So I asked him what he was going to do about it. "I have no choice. I have a family to feed and a child just beginning college. I can't quit. There's nothing I can do to make that much money." His pain was etched in the lines in his face. I felt for him, but I felt much more deeply for the churches he had harmed and would harm by not being an authentic pastor.

Misdirected Story #4

She came up to me after one of my sessions on leadership. I could see I was going to get it, and I did. "I suppose you don't think I'm called to ordained ministry," she quipped. "Tell me why you are in ordained ministry and I'll try to respond," I replied. It turned out she had become ordained in the 1970s because she felt called to champion the cause of feminism. Feminism is a worthy cause, but not a reason to be ordained. I've championed her cause many times in my life, along with Caesar Chavez's grape and lettuce campaign, Martin Luther King Jr. and civil rights, and Saul Alinsky and his confrontation movement. But none of those is a reason to become ordained to pastor a congregation. They may be part of one's ministry as they were mine, but they can never be the reason for being ordained and pastoring a congregation.

So I told her, "No, God didn't call you to pastor a church; God called you to champion a cause. There's quite a difference." A lot of fur flew that afternoon. None of it was useable when it was all over.

So What?

So, what can be done about this mess? It's time we got honest with ourselves. We need to wake up to the fact that God calls Christians to some form of service that has absolutely nothing to do with seminary, formal ordination, or full-time service. When Christians fully understand that God's plan includes everyone doing the actual work of ministry rather than a special few, things will change in our congregations. But more important, lives will cease to be lived without experiencing the joy of reaching God's potential.

Also, I'm convinced that some of the pastors who are not functioning as pastors (that is, they are taking care of the saints instead of equipping them) are doing so because laity have been convinced that caring for people is their pastor's job and the laity are forcing pastors to play "pastor fetch" and private counselor. I want to give these pastors permission to say, *"Enough is enough."* There's still time to get retooled. All you have to do is want to badly enough. If you get retooled and your congregation kicks you out, don't fret; if God called you to be a pastor, there will be another church waiting for you. What you need to remember is there are far more churches now than there are ordained clergy.

A Way Out

If you have decided that you were not called to pastoral ministry and want to do the right thing and find a secular vocation, read appendix 3, which contains two articles by Eddie Hammett, "Alternative Careers for Today's Distressed Clergy" and "Translating Ministry Skills into Alternative Professions (Pathways of Transition for Distressed Clergy)."

REFLECTION TIME

- How did this chapter make you feel? Are you happy with the feeling? If not, why?
- Did any one of the four stories hit home with you? If so, what can you do about it? If not, consider yourself blessed.
- In your journal, record your thoughts about the specifics of your call? What was the central focus of it? Was it generic?
- If you are a denominational leader, what is keeping you from screening candidates for ordination based on Ephesians and their ability to equip rather than one's theological stance or willingness to roll over and play "pastor fetch"?
- Do we still need to talk in terms of clergy and laity?
- If everyone is called by God to some form of ministry, do we really need to ordain people to the special role of pastor? If so, then why not also ordain people to be apostles, prophets, teachers, and evangelists?

CHAPTER SIX

WHAT IF I HAVEN'T YET DISCOVERED MY CALL?

by Linnea Nilsen Capshaw

> *So I hated life, because what is done under the sun was grievous to me; for all is vanity and chasing after wind.* —Ecclesiastes 2:17

When we find our souls filled with frustration and rage over the uselessness of our lives, when all effort seems hopeless and all struggle in vain, when we yearn for purpose and meaning, then we know that we have not yet laid claim to our calling. Mary Ylvisaker Nilsen wrote about calling:

All people have a call from God and we miss out on the divine purpose of our lives if we do not journey through the process to discover it.

We all have been summoned to a vocation, a calling, a task in this world for which we are uniquely qualified. Sometimes that vocation is what we do to earn a living. Often it is not. The call is from God, who needs us to be passionately engaged with the world, working to bring healing and wholeness to all creation. Our call resonates deep within us, interweaving with our gifts and talents in a way that creatively empowers us. We have no road maps, no guides, only a call.

When we hear that call and respond with a hesitant but faithful yes, then rage and frustrations fade, and hope can grow.

May we hear and respond to our calling.[1]

Ten years ago, when I read those words for the first time,

Does your story resonate with my story?

they bored into my soul. I was a young, successful hospital administrator, living the kind of life that most people would envy. But I was wretched. "The problem isn't your job," my brother told me at one point, "it's your spirit." I rejected his analysis, but God kept nudging—or, at times, it felt as if God was hitting me over the head. Life got more and more frustrating. Then I read these words and whispered, "Yes. I want my life to be different. Yes, I want to know what God wants for me. Yes, I am ready."

I would like to tell you that the journey has been easy, that God spoke in a clear voice, that the path I was asked to travel was smooth, that there have always been recognizable guides along the way. But, such is not the case—and we need only look at biblical characters, including Jesus, to know that responding to God's call does not ensure a pain-free life. But I have never regretted that yes—never regretted moving from a driven life to a called life—never regretted setting out on a circuitous journey with only the knowledge that my life is in the hands of a trustworthy

God. In fact, I thank God regularly that I am so privileged to be called to a new way of being and living.

Since that time, I have met many people who are like I was—restless, frustrated, stressed, longing for something different, but who say they don't understand call. Or they don't believe they, too, are called. But they are open, they are willing, and they say yes.

Yes, I Want to Hear My Call. Now What?

For a few fortunate people, the simple assent, saying yes to God, is all that is necessary for them to begin hearing the voice of their Creator calling them to some new way of life. This voice sometimes comes through others, sometimes through reading Scripture or other inspirational writings, sometimes through thoughts and images that come to them in still moments. If you are one of these people, you are ready to begin the discernment process described in the section following titled "Yes, I Want to Respond. Now What?" But for many it is not so easy.

> "Spirit noises" keep us from hearing.

A good friend of mine realized she was missing out on most of what was being said to her, and so, after much resistance, she decided to solve the problem by wearing hearing aids. She thought that as soon as she turned on that aid everyone would sound perfectly clear to her again. However, what she discovered was that the hearing aid didn't allow her to choose whom she wanted to hear. Instead it picked up all the sounds around her, making it nearly impossible to hear anything clearly. It took weeks of experimenting to finally be able to hear what she wanted to hear.

For many of us, our spiritual life is like the process my friend went through: we know we want to hear God more clearly, so we say yes to a "spiritual hearing aid." But a thousand other voices clamor for attention, voices we have repressed for years as we lived our life directed by the loud insistent voice of our culture. These might be the voices of our old angers and resentments that we have allowed to fester in our souls. Or they might be the hurts, often from our childhoods, that we never exposed to healing balm. Or they could be the prejudices and hatreds we have allowed to foment. Or perhaps they are the frustrations and envies, self-pity and self-justification that eat away at our spirit.

When we say yes to God's call, we need to work intentionally to name, tend to, and then quiet all other voices before we can hear the call with clarity.

So what are the noises that block out the voice of God calling you through your spiritual hearing aid to a life of purpose and meaning?

Naming the Distracting Noise in Our Lives

There are at least three types of "spirit noise" that block us from hearing our call from God.

- The chatter of our egos block us from hearing God: "I want to fix the world—or at least *my* world." "I want to be the leader, to be recognized, to be important." "I want a special job, one that I can do by myself."
- The chatter of our angers, resentments, envies, and grief block us from hearing God. These are extremely important voices to listen to. In the "Twelve Steps" of AA and Al-Anon, people are required to do a Fourth Step—a fearless moral inventory. To look at themselves. To listen to all those old tapes and voices— admit them, work them through, and let them go. This is a good model for all of us, for the call of God cannot get through to us if we are clinging to an old grudge or harboring an old wound, or refusing to forgive people, or refusing to walk through the valley of grief for all the losses we have experienced.

• Finally, the chatter of our nagging doubt, insecurity, and lack of trust block us from hearing God. Some doubt God, questioning whether God really loves them, is active in their lives, is for them and not against them. Others doubt themselves: "I'm not good enough, talented enough, strong enough." "I don't have the right gifts, the right education, the right background."

Your chatter may come from issues with your family of origin, from past experiences and choices, from current relationships. The source is not important. What is important is listening to those voices, naming them, and then working to quiet them.

What chatter is stopping you from hearing God's call? Can you identify it? Could close friends help you identify it?

Listening to and Quieting the Distracting Noise

Most of us have some deep pain or longing in our lives that we need to understand and process before we can hear our call, because it is next to impossible to discover your call on top of unexamined pain and longing. Among other things, I was suffering from the pain of believing that I wasn't enough, and I felt like I had to save the world in order to *be enough*. Until I accepted that I *am enough* just as I am, as a child of God, I couldn't hear God's call for the next stage of my life.

Finding a Safe Environment

We cannot do this deep healing work alone. Therefore, it is important to find a safe place where you can trust the other people and open up to them from your heart. Without this element of respect and confidentiality, no process will work for you. You need safe space.

The Faith at Work organization has developed important guidelines for groups to follow in order to create this kind of space. You may find these guidelines helpful in this process. See appendix 4.

There are many places where this work can take place. Find the environment that works best for you.

- You might feel most comfortable in a small group that has been developed through your faith community or a Twelve Step group of some kind.
- Or you might want more one-on-one attention from a spiritual director, counselor, psychiatrist, or clinical social worker.
- You might feel more comfortable in a retreat setting where spiritual work is accomplished. There are many such places across the country.
- Or you may discover settings where therapists incorporate holistic mind/body/spirit experiences or look at the foundations of people's lifestyles.

There are more options than we could imagine or share with you here, so if you are at this place, do a little research, pray, and determine what type of environment may be best for you to examine and process all the distracting noises in your life.

Spending Private Time in Reading, Prayer, and Meditation

We all need to spend time with God alone, but this is particularly important during these times of intense spiritual work.

You can begin your reading in Psalms—a wonderful collection chronicling human suffering and striving for God, and God's response to our striving. A variety of psalms may be helpful: the orientation psalms (praise God, e.g., "Bless the LORD, oh my soul" Psalm 103); the disorientation psalms (e.g., "Why have you forsaken me?" Psalm 88); and the reorientation psalms (e.g., "I've waited for the Lord and he inclined his ear to me" Psalm 55). Read the psalms and find ones that fit you and what you have experienced. Then try writing your own psalm, reflecting on your places of anger, of deep pain, of longing. This process, guided by the Spirit, can help you get in touch with and process the noise that is distracting you from the call of God for your life. Prayer—talking to God—is also a necessary part of this process, and can be done in many ways. However, I am amazed at the number of people who expect the pastor to be their "pray-er" and feel as if they aren't good enough to pray or don't know how to pray.

Think of your relationship to God as similar to your relationship with someone you really care about—perhaps a spouse, a parent, a child. All close relationships depend on spending time together, sharing your thoughts and feelings and listening to the other. There is nothing too unimportant or trivial to talk about with someone you love. In the same way you can talk with God, sharing what's on your mind and in your heart and soul by talking out loud or in silence, singing, or journaling.

Meditation—time spent quietly listening to God—is equally important. Through silence and being present with God, you open yourself up to hearing the still, small voice, the nudge, the random thought that is a "God thought." Stopping for a moment of quiet with God can happen anytime during the day and can be as subtle as a breath prayer—breathing God in, breathing anger out.

And God can also speak to us in Scripture, through a friend's advice, in a book, through music, in nature, through soul cards, in a labyrinth, through an on-line chat. I have found this to be one of the most challenging and rewarding experiences: being silent before God and open to God's voice coming to me through unexpected channels.

My spiritual director shared a motto that we should spend at least one hour a day, one day a week, and one week a year in intentional time with God, reading, reflecting, listening, and being. This may seem like a lofty goal, but it may be just what you need in order to quiet all the distracting voices and hear your call from God to a fulfilling life on earth!

Yes, I Want to Respond. Now What?

If necessary, you have gone through the long and painful process of paying attention to God and asking God's help in releasing all those noises that keep you from hearing the call of God. And you have felt a nudge in a certain direction.

My first big nudge came after reading Bob Buford's book, *Halftime*. At that time, I felt God was calling me to a life in which I would work in health care half of my time and work in the church or for other kinds of mission enterprises the other half. How could I know whether this was really God's voice or the voice of my ego, again, pushing me to do something I would get recognition for?

The Servant Leadership School helps us understand that there are four marks of our call from God:

1. Always a simple statement.
2. Always impossible to do on our own.
3. Not ego-driven/one's own invention.
4. Strange persistence to the call.

For me, it was a simple statement: use your gifts to build God's kingdom on earth. Yet, it was impossible to do on my own. In fact, I started out with two partners to consult and coach as I developed my company because I knew I couldn't do it alone. What I discovered, after those two people within months were called to other vocations, was that God wanted me to rely on God alone—not other people! I must confess that my ego was fed much more as a hospital administrator than as one leaving that job to start a business. Most people thought I was crazy, since I had never done anything like that before, was only thirty years old and was leaving the security of a well-paying job for no security at all. However, the call wouldn't let go of me. I had huge fears about doing this, I had people tell me it was too risky, I had only a small amount of savings in the bank before I would have to access my retirement funds—but the call wouldn't let go of me. And that's one of the constants of any call—it won't go away! I just had to do something to use my gifts to build God's kingdom on earth!

To hear our call, it is often helpful to identify our spiritual gifts, passions, personality styles, talents and skills, so we know how God has uniquely wired us. When I realized that I had leadership, administration skills, and faith as my top three spiritual gifts, I was amazed! I had been using all those gifts in my career, but did not understand until that time that they were spiritual gifts from God that I could use to further God's purposes on earth. There are many tools now to facilitate this learning.[2] It is often helpful to get feedback from others who know you well once you have completed one of these assessments to help you discern your gifts.

Keep in mind, however, we also learn through biblical stories that there is no clear correlation between gifts and call. For example, Moses was called by God to free the Israelites from Egypt, which required that he speak boldly to the Pharaoh. However, Moses kept telling God that he wasn't the man for the job because he was "slow of speech and slow of tongue." After much persistence, God finally allowed Moses' brother Aaron to go with him to do the speaking for Moses. God called Moses to a role for which he had no natural gifts. Our call may not coincide with our gifts either—a situation that truly makes us dependent upon God and other human beings.

Discerning How to Respond to the Call

After such a process, you may want to gather a discernment group to begin to help you figure out just exactly what this call means, what you should do now, what concrete steps you should take. *Listening Hearts: Discerning Call in Community* is a great resource for this process.[3] The basics of a discernment group consist of the following:

- Share the issue prior to meeting with approximately three discerners and the group spends time in prayer.
- Gather for prayer, not discussion, and listen and wait for God to speak through the group.
- After introductions, spend time in silence.
- Discerners then ask simple questions only after quiet reflection so people can discern; they do not give advice or make decisions. Questions should help the person move toward clarity of God's call.
- Spend more time in silence throughout the gathering.
- Thirty minutes before the end of the designated time, allow the focus person to ask questions of the group.
- Set another meeting if needed and close in prayer.
- Continue to be in prayer afterward for the person to refine his or her discernment process and hear clearly from God.

For another discernment resource, the Shalem Institute for Spiritual Formation in Bethesda, Maryland has developed a group spiritual direction training course and process to help people hear God's call for their lives on an ongoing basis in a small group community setting.[4]

For many people, there is a significant moment in life when they hear their call from God and begin the process of responding to that call. I used to regularly share with people how I "heard my call" from God as I read the book *Halftime.* Eight years later, I have realized that my call from God consists of more than a one time event, more than just the way I organize my working life. It has to do with all of me, for all of life as I journey with God: my career, my family, my friends, my faith community, my goals and dreams. Like the voice of a shepherd calling his sheep, the voice of God comes daily in little and big ways, nudging, directing, redirecting—and sometimes it is a sharp voice, stopping me from taking a particularly dangerous turn.

Marjorie Bankson in her book *The Call to the Soul* describes a cycle that we experience as we hear and respond to call and she shares that we may journey through this cycle a number of times in our lifetime as we are called to different phases of our lives.[5]

> Have you heard your call yet?

Most important, we must understand that we *all* have a call from God and that we miss out on the divine purpose of our lives if we do not journey through the process to discover this call. No, it won't be easy. Yes, it will be worth it! You will discover your purpose, your reason for being, your unique role and call to help transform this world to one of faith, hope, and love. May you discover your call in this life.

REFLECTION TIME

• Have you discovered your call from God?
• If not, what are the noises that get in your way of hearing God even with your spiritual hearing aid turned on?
• What type of safe-space environment do you think would work best for you to tend to the distracting noises and to further pursue your call?
• How can you continually improve your time alone talking to God?
• Have you identified your gifts, passion, and personality style and begun to pray about how they may interweave with your call from God?
• Have you asked God to provide for you a discernment group that can help you hear and refine your call from God?
• Remember that appendix 4, "Faith at Work Guidelines for Groups," was offered in this chapter.

Notes

1. Mary Ylvisaker Nilsen, *A Time for Peace: Daily Meditations for Twelve-step Living* (Iowa City: Zion Publishing, 1990), November 2.
2. Some of the best resources to facilitate learning about spiritual gifts are: *Discovering Your Place in God's World*, Bill Easum & Linnea Nilsen Capshaw, Network by Network Ministries,

PLACE by Place Ministries, SHAPE by Saddleback Community Church.

3. Suzanne G. Farnham, Joseph P. Gill, R. Taylor McLean, and Susan M. Ward, *Listening Hearts: Discerning Call in Community* (Harrisburg, Pa.: Morehouse Publishing, 1991).

4. Shalem Institute for Spiritual Formation, Bethesda, Maryland, www.shalem.org.

5. Marjorie Bankson, *The Call to the Soul* (Philadelphia: Innisfree Press, 1999).

Preferred Leadership Style Exercise

Before reading the next chapter, take a brief moment to do this exercise. It will prepare you for the chapter to follow. The following exercise is to pinpoint the two things about your ministry that light your fire. Choose two, and only two, statements that best describe your style of ministry.

1. "I have a driving passion to see people become committed followers of Jesus Christ."
2. "I enjoy visiting people in parishioners' homes, hospitals, and nursing homes and giving people spiritual comfort."
3. "I enjoy managing the institution so that it remains in good order for the sake of the present and future members."
4. "I'm willing to try anything that isn't biblically immoral, even if it is illegal, if it will help my church expand its influence and reach more people."
5. "Since we've never done this ministry before, it must be what we need to do. If it doesn't work, so what? We will learn from it for the next attempt."
6. "My passion in life is to oversee a kingdom movement that will result in the multiplication of congregations to the point that the Great Commission is fulfilled in my lifetime."

My choices are _____

CHAPTER SEVEN

FIVE LEADERSHIP STYLES: WHICH ONE MATCHES YOUR CALL?

Bob was a regular participant in one of our online mentoring forums.[1] He was the pastor of a church that had been declining for decades and he had been struggling to turn it around. I never met anyone who cared more deeply about his leadership than Bob. He was constantly working to improve his ministry and turn his church around. But no matter what he tried, nothing changed. Bob was gifted; he cared deeply; he worked hard; but still the church declined.

Six months into our relationship, it became clear to both of us that Bob had to deal with his high mercy gift if he was going to be a turnaround pastor. Two mean-spirited folks tightly controlled every decision made in the church. Every time a new initiative began to gain momentum, these two would scuttle it. And Bob was unable to stand up to them and keep them from intimidating the church.

Bob had to make a decision—either change his preferred style of leadership or give up his dream of turning that church around. The clash between his passion for transformation and the frustration brought about by one failure after the other finally got the best of Bob. One day he just quit. Bob is now a very effective chaplain in a denominational hospital.

Here is his last communication with me about six months after he became a chaplain.

Subject: **Thanks**
Date: 5/30/2001 11:18:35 AM Eastern Standard Time
From: Bob@whoguessedit.com
To: Easum

Thanks for coaching me through this situation—when I asked why my church didn't move ahead more quickly, I had to look in the mirror. It took me a long time to realize the truth—the more entrenched a church is, the more the leadership of the pastor is going to be put to the test. And some churches' ability to resist will be greater than a pastor's passion or ability to move it ahead. That's my case. My style of leadership just won't cause it to happen. The more I examine my call, the more I realize that God really called and gifted me to be a caregiver more than a pastor. Now that I am where I was called to be, I've never been happier.
Thanks.
Bob

Understanding your leadership style preference is crucial to self-fulfillment as a leader. Sometimes our call and our preferred style of leadership naturally match. What a blessing. However, sometimes they are a mismatch. When that happens, we have a choice. We can do whatever is necessary to change our preferred style to match the specifics of our call, or we can live with the frustrating and often debilitating consequences of our preferred style.

I should mention at this point, that I am not equating style with gifts. For example: the gift of administration is a valid gift, but the managerial style that I will explain later is not valid as a preferred style of leadership.

In my travels I've experienced five types of preferred leadership styles. Four of these styles are valid calls from God; one isn't. Only three of these styles naturally lead and grow individuals and congregations. As we examine these styles, keep in mind that they can be quite mixed, so the key for you is to see which one best describes your normal behavior. Then you must ask, Will my preferred style of leadership help or hinder the fulfillment of my call?

Enabler

I received the following e-mail from a pastor who I never met but who had read some of my books.

Subject:	**What should I do?**
Date:	1/3/2000 3:18:35 AM Eastern Standard Time
From:	Dude@squarten.com
To:	Easum

> My heart aches for my church. I want so badly to help it turn itself around and start growing again, but I don't seem to have the ability to do so. Turning it around would cause us to make so many difficult decisions, and most of them would cause some deep hurt within the congregation. It might even break up some friendships. I don't like conflict and I certainly don't like hurting people. But I want so much to help advance the kingdom. What should I do?

My distant friend's frustration is due to his call not matching his preferred leadership style. My friend is an enabler. Enablers are people who above all else love caring for people so passionately that transformation or discipleship is seldom a concern. They often exude the Great Commandment, often to the extent that they have no time left for the Great Commission. Because they care so deeply about how others feel, they usually:

- Allow everyone else to set their agenda instead of letting the call set it
- Wait for problems to come to them instead of anticipating the problem
- Avoid controversy rather than address it
- Wait to take action until they are forced, instead of being proactive

Often, this desire to care goes to the point that the enabler depends on his or her church to need him or her. In the most severe cases, the enabler needs the church to need him or her in order to gain self-worth.

Enablers usually have such a high level of mercy in their personality or gift mix that they render themselves ineffective. All of us have some mercy in us. The key is, does our tendency toward mercy dominate our lives? Mother Teresa had great mercy, but also great leadership skills and used her mercy to fuel her mission. Mercy is good if it fuels the mission; it is disastrous if it stifles or sidetracks it. With most enablers, mercy derails the mission.

The statement in the opening exercise that best defines enablers is: "I enjoy visiting people in parishioners' homes, hospitals, and nursing homes and giving people spiritual comfort." If you checked this one, your preferred leadership style is probably that of an enabler. But here are a few more statements that can help you determine if you are an enabler. Each one is a mercy statement. As you will see, they are excellent statements for one to make. The issue is, how much do these kinds of statements give primary direction to your ministry? The more they do, the less effective you are likely to be as a leader.

- I often get frustrated when I see people hurt, displaced, or rejected.
- I find it hard to terminate someone's employment.
- I can easily look beyond a person's inadequacies or problems and see a life that matters.

- I feel such compassion for hurting people that I actively do what I can to alleviate the sources of their pain.
- I work through relationships rather than information to help people find wholeness in their lives.
- I go out of my way to avoid conflict.

Enabling is a valid gift from God and my comments should not in any way be seen as derogatory. If you're an enabler, don't give up just yet. According to a study done by George Barna, 35 percent of the effective transformational leaders have a high mercy gift.[2] So, even though it's hard for you to lead, you can.

> **Enablers are seldom transformers or effective as leaders.**

When enablers are able to lead, they have learned to either overcome or compensate for their preferred style of leadership. What I see effective enablers doing most often is gathering around themselves a group of more entrepreneurial types and allowing one of them to assume the role of executive pastor who handles the difficult issues, many of which will involve staffing. Sort of like the team of Moses, Aaron, and Jethro.

If you fall into this category but it does not fit your call or you want to change your preferred style of leadership, read appendix 5, "Changing Your Enabler Style."

Let me say a final word to those who feel called and gifted to be a caregiver, counselor, or enabler. If you're comfortable with your leadership preference being that of an enabler, don't be surprised or hurt if you are unable to be a transformational leader who brings people to Christ, turns a church around, starts a new church, leads an exciting ministry in your church, or is on the cutting edge of the future. To do so, you will have to change or compensate for your style and that can be truly painful. You can change only if you want to. However, you may be called to be an

81

enabler and if so, the odds are that whatever congregation you serve or ministry you lead will never reach its potential and most will continue to decline.

If you are a pastor, many organizations, other than congregations, need you. Start looking around for a place to authentically follow your call. You might be surprise what doors might open for you, other than pastoring a church.

Managerial and Professional

Managerial and professional types take most of their cues from the last fifty years of modernity and function more like CEO's or COO's than transformational leaders. They take great care in running the church, managing the organization, often to the point of micromanaging the church.

Managerial and professional types don't belong in ministry.

Procedure and proper theology occupy most of their attention. Pastors place great emphasis in their education and official role as the ordained leader of the church. Laity enjoy playing the church game—sitting on committees and applying Robert's Rules of Order.

Participating in the activities and ministries of the larger church is high on their agenda. Often they are overdependent on their religious affiliation and are seen as company men and women. Pastors use denominational events as a way to get away from the responsibilities in their congregation. Laity see denominational events or structures as another opportunity to wield power and control.

The statement that best defines their ministry is: "I enjoy managing the institution so that it remains in good order for the sake of the present and future members."

At their best, managerial and professionals are spiritual infants; at their worst, they are controlling Pharisees or little more than career-oriented ladder climbers. This style will have the most difficult time being an effective leader the farther we go into the twenty-first century since the emerging world wants gifted and authentic amateurs, not academic, professional experts. I have not seen any leadership capacity in the church well served by this style. It is one of the most destructive forms of leadership in the church today. If you are a layperson and fit this category, you probably spend a lot of time trying to control everything that happens in your church and by doing so stifle the work of the Spirit.

If you fall into this category, do yourself and the kingdom a favor and either grow up spiritually, find another profession, or get out of the church. If you are serious about growing up, you might try to plug into our Track One coaching in our Easum, Bandy, and Associates (EBA) Community at www.easumbandy.com. We have helped many managerial types grow and assume transformational roles.

Transformational Leaders

An emerging group of leaders has been forming over the past two decades. I wrote about them in *Leadership on the OtherSide* where I referred to them as "spiritual guides." These Transformational leaders demonstrate the Great Commandment by leading the church to carry out the Great Commission. Transformational leaders have the style of leadership that is most needed in the

> **Transformational Leaders**
>
> • Adaptive
> • Breakthrough
> • Apostolic

church at any time in history. Their goal is to transform individuals and society into followers of Jesus Christ.

Transformational leaders fall into three categories: adaptive, breakthrough, and apostolic. Their common traits are:

83

- They are *passionate* followers of Jesus Christ.
- Their chief goal is to equip disciples to reproduce themselves.
- They are *rabidly* focused on their mission and flexible on most other issues.
- They *trust* and *act on* their intuitions as they explore the edges of normalcy looking for the next innovation.
- They model servanthood rather than professionalism.
- They act as spiritual midwives helping others birth their God-given gifts.
- They have a common prayer that seems to permeate all that they do and are: "Show me what you are doing in this world. Put me in the midst of it. Run over me with your presence and allow me to be part of your great movement on earth."

All three of these transformational styles find their expression in the following statements:

- "I often influence others to be more than they thought they could be."
- "I can live with disagreement and diversity of thought as long as the mission is being accomplished. I am a big-picture thinker and effectively share vision with others."
- "I can guide others to achieve goals or change systems in such a way that they feel as if they are led by the Spirit."
- "Teams that I have mentored have grown and sensed God's presence."
- "I have a consuming passion to reach non-Christians."
- "When I share my personal story and faith, people often respond positively by accepting Jesus."
- "I like to motivate others to take more seriously the relationship between their faith and how they live."

He's a bit biased + + probably ecumenical ok ux doctrinal gray s to a liberal? bent.

If after finishing this chapter, you find that you fall into one of the transformational categories but find that you are still bothered a bit by your mercy gift, read appendix 6, "The Problem with Mercy Gifts."

Adaptive

Adaptive leaders are skilled at seeing what others are doing and learning from them. They aren't afraid to try new things, nor do they limit their scope of inquiry to their denomination or group. They're constantly searching the landscape for effective ministries they feel could be adapted to their church setting. I counsel this kind of leader to attend or visit at least two conferences or innovative congregations a year to see what God is doing and to ask, "What will work back home if I tweak it?"

> **Adaptive leaders learn from others and adapt to their setting.**

These leaders focus on developing thriving congregations where people are growing in their spiritual development as well as affecting the values of the outside community. They usually see their role and responsibility as defined by their local congregation.

This style of leadership is best suited for turning a church around or taking a growing church to the next level, or starting serious new ministries that will change the face of the congregation. To see more information, go to appendix 7, "Turnaround Leaders."

The statement that best defines their ministry is: "I'm willing to try anything that isn't biblically immoral, even if it is illegal, if it will help my church expand its influence and reach more people."

Breakthrough

I first called these leaders "future active" in *How to Reach Baby Boomers* because of their ability to read the signs of the times. A couple of years later I referred to them as "fringe leaders" in *Dancing with Dinosaurs* because not only were they reading the signs of the times, but also they were so far out on the edge that their actions scared a lot of established Christians. They weren't doing much ministry like it used to be done. I wrote in-depth about the character of these leaders in *Leadership on the OtherSide*.

Breakthrough leaders are innovators whose ministries set the stage for future congregational ministries in other churches. They never stifle a new idea. Other pastors often think of them as mavericks, especially if they are within a mainline group.

> **Break-through leaders set the pace for adaptive leaders.**

They have such a passion for being on the road to mission with Jesus that they will try almost anything, as long as it does not violate their core beliefs, their DNA, and promises to enhance the mission, even if it violates denomination or congregational polity. Most of the ministries of the adaptive leaders come from these breakthrough leaders.

Breakthrough leaders have several common traits:

- Breakthrough leaders always have a kingdom mentality. They see Christianity as a movement and are unshakably committed to fulfilling the Great Commission through their church or its influence in other churches.
- Mission is the mother of their theology.
- They gather information from a vast variety of disciplines.
- They are open to the movement of the Holy Spirit and act fast and decisively when they feel led.
- They practice triage—they work with those who are ready and never the entire church.
- They not only embrace change, they can't live without it.

• They are consumed by a specific call from God, as opposed to a generic call.

The statement that best defines breakthrough leaders is: "Since we've never done this before, it must be what we need to do. If it doesn't work, so what? We'll learn from it and apply it to the next perceived movement of the Spirit."

Apostolic

Until recently, the role of apostolic leader has been used on a limited basis or confined to the first century. However, during the 1990s a growing number of pastors began assuming the biblical role of apostleship. They are assuming leadership over a large number of new church plants or multiple sites that grow out of one congregation. I write about this emerging breed of leader and give numerous examples in my book *Beyond the Box*.

> Apostolic leaders set the pace for building the kingdom and mentoring breakthrough leaders.

Apostolic leaders take the kingdom and movement mentality to its zenith by: starting several multiple sites throughout their city; cutting themselves loose to function more as the mentor of the campus pastors; and developing church planting centers within each congregation.

Apostolic leaders exhibit a passion for the fulfillment of the Great Commission and participation in the expansion of God's kingdom. They are seldom, if ever, concerned about denominational issues. When they are, it is always how they can partner with and mentor sister congregations.

Apostolic leaders have the following common characteristics:

- Their passion for the kingdom causes them to begin exercising influence over more than just one church or area.
- Methodology is relatively unimportant compared to one driving passion—does it transform people and community?
- They have radically decentralized everything in order to facilitate the exponential exploration of new and better ways to expand the kingdom.
- Rather than developing programs to involve people, these leaders focus on intensive, on-the-job modeling of everyone in their congregation.
- Mission dictates their partnerships.

The statement that best defines their ministry is: "My passion in life is to oversee a kingdom movement that will result in the multiplication of congregations to the point that the Great Commission is fulfilled in my lifetime."

This group is the smallest of all effective Christians I have met and virtually none of them fall within the mainline camp—yet. However, I expect this category to be the fastest growing of the five leadership styles over the next few decades.

What a Leader Lives For

The following e-mail came to me from a recent participant in one of my "Put On Your Own Oxygen Mask First" seminars where we go through much of the material in this book. Listen to his story and see if you can find yourself in it. This e-mail is made of the stuff for which I live.

Subject: **What I learned**
Date: 5/30/2003 3:40:21 PM Pacific Standard Time
From: Tom@youwhotee.com
To: Easum

Some of what I experienced last week with you has to do with the concern over having to change styles in order to move the mission ahead. I now have an inkling why I almost walked out on ministry ten years ago. So many people affirmed my chaplaincy skills. But my heart was yearning for something else that it didn't feel I had permission to pursue. Call it weakness, or maybe just naiveté, but I allowed the pressure of peers and system to form me into a mold that chafed my soul. What I'm sensing from my 1 and 5 choices is this: I no longer need to be embarrassed or ashamed that I DON'T LIKE TO VISIT HOMES, HOSPITALS OR NURSING HOMES! Even now, as I type this, a little voice in the back of my mind is saying, "But you're a PASTOR, and that's what pastors do!" I am so discovering, and enjoying, the empowerment that comes with telling that damnable little voice to get lost!

Could this e-mail be expressing how you feel?

REFLECTION TIME

- How are you feeling at this point? Write it down in your journal. Pray over it as long as you need. This could be an important juncture in your life.
- Take all the time you need at this point to focus on the compatibility of your call and your preferred leadership style. Do they match?
- If you are a pastor, who in your congregation needs to join you in reading this book and implementing the findings?
- If you are a layperson, who do you know that would benefit from this book?
- Now, it's time to begin the hard work.
- Remember that three appendixes were offered in this chapter: appendix 5, "Changing Your Enabler Style," appendix 6, "The Problem with Mercy Gifts," and appendix 7, "Turnaround Leaders."

Notes

1. For more information on my mentoring forums, go to www.easumbandy.com.
2. Barna Research Online, www.barna.org.

SECTION 3
EFFECTIVE LEADERSHIP

Does Your Context Fit Your Call
and Style?

Does Your Skill Set Match
Your Call?

My Personal Mission Statement

CHAPTER EIGHT

DOES YOUR CONTEXT FIT YOUR CALL AND STYLE?

One of the keys to effective and authentic leadership is to match the context of the ministry to your call and preferred style of leadership.

A friend of mine is the lead pastor of a five-year-old church plant that already has over two thousand people in worship. What's really interesting about his story is that this is his second plant. His first plant failed to get off the ground.

What made the difference? The second time around he was very careful to make sure the context of the new plant matched his style and call. What did he do the second time? He visited city after city to evaluate the following:

- Where are the cities with the demographics that my style and call can best reach?
- What kind of ministry are the churches in the area not doing effectively?
- Does the nonexistent ministry fit my preferred style, call, and skill set?
- Is the city one in which I could live for the next twenty years?
- Is God calling me to transform this city?

When all of the data was compiled, he knew that he had a reasonable chance at an effective and authentic ministry.

I have an apostolic style of leadership coupled sometimes with a "thus saith the Lord" approach. I came into all four churches I pastored casting a vision the first Sunday and letting people know where I was going if they wanted to join me. Needless to say that won't work in every context, as proved by the fact that I was fired from my first church!

Be Careful Here

Even though the context in which you find yourself may have a bearing on the effectiveness of your ministry, great care must be exercised at this point. You must never make the mistake of quickly blaming the context for a failure. That's too easy a way out. Transformational leaders never blame the system or the context, instead they take full responsibility for the situation in which they find themselves. They exercise their call no matter what the circumstances.

> Don't take the easy way out and blame the context.

I pastored my fourth and last church for twenty-four years. When I went there, I was told the church was a losing proposition because two of the very best pastors of our denomination had failed. They gave me a choice—bury or resurrect it. To my superiors it looked like a sow's ear; to me it looked like a silk purse. The situation was so bad I could have easily buried it. But I knew two things about the context that made me believe I could resurrect that church: one, the makeup of the two previous pastors did not match the people in the area; and two, there were more than 500,000 people within ten miles of the church. I dug in to stay.

Where Does Your Style Best Fit?

Even though context is one of the wide variables in leadership, it is possible to make the following comments about matching call, style, and context.

- Enablers work best in dying churches, hospices, and hospitals. To put an enabler in a turnaround or growth situation is to cause a lot of misery for a lot of people, especially the enabler. Enablers usually shrink a church down to a size they can handle.
- Managerial and professionals shouldn't be in a leadership position, period.
- Adaptive leaders work best in thriving situations where growth potential exists for both the institution and individuals. However, I see far too many adaptive leaders stuck in bad contexts. They want the church to grow, but the leaders don't or won't make the necessary changes to make growth possible. One of two things always happens: enormous conflict erupts or the adaptive leader shuts down and drifts away from his or her call. The greatest joys of my ministry are the many notes and e-mails I receive from pastors thanking me for stirring up their call and giving them permission to lead rather than follow someone else's agenda.
- Breakthrough leaders work best in new situations or in congregations on the cutting edge in ministry. Often these folks are leaders of teaching churches. Breakthrough leaders don't waste time in dead end situations. Most of them have either left their denomination or were never part of one. Those who have stayed in a denomination are clearly identifiable as different.

- Apostolic leaders hit their prime when they have oversight for more than one church by either birthing a church-planting movement or developing multiple sites, or by becoming a mentor to many congregations. Some forms of apostolic leaders are consultants to a wide range of leaders. Seldom does this type of leader enjoy working within the confines of one denomination or group.

Not as Neat as It Looks

It is quite possible for these five styles to be mixed together. A person may have some of each style or a little of one style and a lot of another. On top of that, the context can have a large bearing not only on how effective a leader might be, but also on how the leader might have to function to fulfill the call long term.

In our online EBA Community[1] it is my custom to allow the members of the community to preview my books as they are being written and make comments and suggestions. Here is an e-mail that began a conversation around the issue of style and context.

Subject: **[advanced-leadership] Re: Continuum?**
Date: 6/7/2003 7:38:00 AM Eastern Standard Time
From: Sally@rand.com
To: Easum

Bill and all,
These five descriptions are quite helpful and accurate. They seem to be on a continuum of an effective change agent. For instance, enabler is the least effective and apostle will have the greatest impact on world transformation. I believe we know that we're not devaluing any of them, but just squaring with the reality of the type of leader it takes for kingdom

results. I see pastors in nearly all established mainline churches as having to go through all five stages beginning with the enabler. I guess that very few ever make it from enabler to apostle, the stretch is just too great. If a pastor plants a church, he or she can begin as a transformational leader, perhaps even bypassing the adaptive form of it.

But in a church turnaround, if you arrive and the church expects you to be their enabler or administrator, you probably have to pass through all stages. I know that when I arrived at the church that I equip, after about six months I realized that the newer members on the search committee brought me in to be transformational (adaptive type), the church board wanted me to be managerial, and the church grassroots wanted an enabler. Boy, don't you know that sparks flew because my heart was into the breakthrough type of leader.

After almost five years, I am now at the adaptive stage just inching into the breakthrough.

Sally

Subject:	**[advanced-leadership] Re: Continuum?**
Date:	6/7/2003 1:12:00 PM Eastern Standard Time
From:	Easum
To:	Sally@rand.com

Sally brings up an interesting point. Does everyone have to go through the stages? Although it was not my intention to suggest a continuum, I can see how that might happen to some. It did for Sally. The key for Sally is "Are you able to retire where you are?" If not, you will probably have to start over again and that will be painful. In Sally's case it has taken her five years to get to the adaptive stage, but she has not lost her job.

However, it has been my experience that most leaders don't do what Sally did and that the first four types are not a continuum. Most effective leaders hit the ground using their preferred style and if successful, never change.

Yet, the more I look at this the more I see wisdom in what Sally is saying. I just considered my own style. Although I never played the enabler game, I did start out as adaptive for a very short time, say four years, and then became breakthrough the rest of my pastoral ministry. So, I can see how there was some progression.

But I must make this point. The managerial style is never a good or biblical style and must be avoided. I can see going from enabler to adaptive, as long as the managerial is bypassed.

One of the things I'm trying to stress in this material is that the more the context changes one's basic calling the more likely one of the following will happen: the pastor will become what the congregation wants for the rest of the pastor's life and give up the call; the pastor will drop out of ministry; the pastor will become bitter and continue till there is a way out. Historically, if you look at what has happened, very few pastors have survived allowing the setting to redirect their basic calling. Most give in over time. This is why I like Friedman [Edwin Friedman, rabbi and author] so much. He suggests that one should always set one's own agenda and when one doesn't, the odds are stacked against him or her.

Sally, you seem to have survived the continuum. You're one of the blessed ones.

Bill

The Rare Exception

Of course, some contexts do exist where no matter what a person does, nothing will change. Here are some examples of contexts that might be worth leaving:

98

- Congregations located in areas from which most of the people have moved.
- Congregations with a family system so dysfunctional that it would take the death of most of the leaders for the church to have a chance. If you decide this is the context, read appendix 8, "The Small Dysfunctional Church," before deciding to bail out.
- If you are a blue collar person in a white collar church or vice versa.
- Congregations that don't want to do anything but rot!
- Congregations where almost all of the people are related to one another.

If you are in one of these rare situations, you might think about moving if you are a transformational leader.

REFLECTION TIME

- Is the context you are in now one in which you feel you can effectively live out your calling? If so, what is it you lack in your skill set? If not, why and what can you do about it?
- If you've concluded the context doesn't fit your call and preferred style, what criteria are you using to determine how long you should stay in this context?
- What logic or exercise have you used to determine if the context matches your call or preferred style?
- In your journal, make a list of the pros and cons of your present context. Pray over each of them to see what insights might come to you.
- Remember that this chapter contains a reference to appendix 8, "The Small Dysfunctional Church."

Note

1. To see what the EBA Community offers, go to www.easumbandy.com and click on "Join the EBA Community."

CHAPTER NINE

DOES YOUR SKILL SET MATCH YOUR CALL?

I've said it many times—I hire for passion and character more than for skill. As a lead pastor, I found it was impossible to teach passion and character, but it was possible to teach skills to passionate people with character. Most of this book has focused on developing an authentic leadership style that fits your call. Now we must focus on the skills of effective leadership that build on the power of authentic leadership. My intent is to give a thumbnail description of each skill and to point you to resources that can help you develop the skills you need to be a transformational leader. The skill set and the amount of training you need obviously depend on more things than can be addressed in this book. What you need to do is decide where your skills need sharpening and dig into the resources listed in that category. I consider the following list of the skills to be essential for leadership in the coming decades.

What Skills Do I Need to Learn?

Traditional Skills	Emerging Skills
Expository Preaching	Motivational Storytelling
European Theology	Apostolic Faith
Confirmation Class Teaching	Core Leadership Coaching
Congregational Programming	Culture of Equipping
Institutional Administration	Decentralized Administration
Strategic Planning	Ministry Mapping
Hierarchical Accountability	Congregational Identity Building
Committee Development	Mission Team Development
Sacramental Uniformity	Discernment of Spirit in Culture
Ability to Use 16th Century Technology	Ability to Use Constantly Updateable Technologies
One-to-one Ministry	Multiplication of Ministry
Large Group Management	Multiplication of Groups
Teaching	Mentoring
Property Management	Community Development
Ecumenical Cooperation	City-Reaching Movements
Professional Development	Faith Models
Evangelism Programs	Lifestyle Evangelism
Membership Assimilation	Gift Discernment

Motivational Storytelling

The day of oral tradition is back. E-mail is seeing to that. Today, people learn more through well-told stories than through the old fact-and-lecture method. Personal stories are often the best at getting a point across. Many churches are now reverting to using personal testimonies from parishioners as part of the worship message. One of the most widely used church curriculum, Promiseland, is built around storytelling. Of course, telling personal stories flies in the face of what most pastors were taught in seminary and what most established curriculum is based on today.

Resources

- Brian D. McLaren, *A New Kind of Christian* (San Francisco: Jossey-Bass, 2001)
- Brian D. McLaren, *The Story We Find Ourselves In* (San Francisco: Jossey-Bass, 2003)
- To learn more about Promiseland, go to http://willowcreek.org/promiseland.asp. To purchase it go to http://www.willowcreek.com/promiseland/curriculum/.

Apostolic Faith

The further we go into the twenty-first century, the more important it will be for Christian leaders to know how to interact with non-Christians who are in an environment that is unfriendly toward Christianity or agnostic. One of the places to learn how to live out the faith in such times is the writings of the Apostolic Fathers. Two realities make the writings of the Apostolic Fathers crucial to effective ministry: first, the twenty-first century will be more like the first century than the twentieth century; and second, during Christendom, Christianity was so compromised and altered that it lost its way. The Reformation and Vatican II were both a step in the right direction, but neither went far enough to radically embrace the faith of the first three centuries.

Resources

- J. B. Lightfoot, *The Apostolic Fathers* (Grand Rapids: Baker Book House, 1956)
This classic on the Apostolic Fathers is out of print but still available in used form at www.amazon.com.
- G. B. Caird, *The Apostolic Age* (London: Duckworth, 1974)
- Walter Elwell and Robert Yarbrough, eds., *Readings from the First-century World* (Grand Rapids: Baker, 1998)
- Rod Bennett, *Four Witnesses* (San Francisco: Ignatius Press, 2002)

Core Leadership Coaching

Perhaps the most important thing a leader does today is to gather and coach a core team of adult leaders. The effective pastors with whom I work tell me they spend the vast majority of their time in the selection, training, and mentoring of this group of leaders. I've noticed that the major mistake of turnaround pastors is the failure to gather and mentor a team at the beginning of the turnaround. Effective and authentic leaders realize that the church isn't based on democratic principles and that the fewer people the leaders work with the stronger the congregation will be over time. The key is to take a core team deep and then have structures in place for that core to replicate itself throughout every level of the congregation.

Resources

- Bill Easum, *Strategic Strategies for Change* (workbook) (Port Aransas, Tex.: EBA, 2002)

Available on http://www.easumbandy.com, under "Workbooks."

- Thomas G. Bandy, *Coaching Change* (Nashville: Abingdon Press, 2000)
  This resource contains a section on how to develop core leaders.

Culture of Equipping

Instead of trying to promote programs, coordinate volunteers, find people to carry out the church programs, or even develop the key leaders of the church, effective leaders put systems in place that develop leaders at every level of the congregation. Effective leaders create equipping cultures where all believers are actively involved in equipping and encouraging each other in this mission with God. They create development experiences at multiple levels. For example, they have ministries for first-time guests, new Christians, and various degrees of maturing Christians. In addition, they have processes in place to move people from the marketplace to the mission field, from less to more responsibility, even to the point of bringing the more committed and gifted ones onto the staff.

Resources

- Bill Easum and Dave Travis, *Beyond the Box* (Loveland, Colo.: Group, 2003), pp. 45-66
- Sue Mallory, *The Equipping Church* (Grand Rapids: Zondervan, 2001)
- Sue Mallory, *The Equipping Church Guidebook* (Grand Rapids: Zondervan, 2001)
- Greg Ogden, *Unfinished Business*, rev. ed. (Grand Rapids: Zondervan, 2003)

Decentralized Administration

Instead of coordinating from the center and on behalf of the institution, effective leaders allow people to lead from the fringes of the congregation. The key is to decentralize authority and power and release people to find their place within the Body rather than trying to coordinate what and how people serve the institution. For decentralization to happen effectively, three things must happen: the congregation must be clear on its mission and identity; the staff must be willing to give up ministry and be willing to mentor; and the congregation must give up micromanaging the day-to-day decisions. I have seen the process begin in stuck churches by the pastor simply beginning to give people permission to attempt new ministries without running it by the "powers that be."

Resources

- William Easum, *Sacred Cows Make Gourmet Burgers* (Nashville: Abingdon Press, 1995)
- Ron Ashkenas, *Boundaryless Organization,* 2d ed. (San Francisco: Jossey-Bass, 1996)

Ministry Mapping

Our world is moving far too fast for leaders to continue long-term strategic planning. Strategic mapping is starting out on the journey with a general idea of where you want to go, yet being flexible enough to be inspired, take detours, reroute, or even start over again if that is where God is leading. Ministry mappers are more like cartographers than planners. They draw topographic maps, not road maps. Instead of setting a five-year plan in concrete and adding to it each year so that a five-year plan is always in place, effective leaders have a destination in mind and do whatever is necessary to reach that destination. Strategic mapping allows for constant flux and adaptation, whereas strategic planning often binds people up in a strategy that doesn't work but everyone feels obliged to continue to honor because so much time went into the planning process.

Resources

- Bill Easum, *Strategic Mapping* (workbook) Published by EBA, www.easumbandy.com, under "Workbooks."
- Thomas G. Bandy, *Moving Off the Map* (Nashville: Abingdon Press, 1998), pp. 245-78

Congregational Identity Building

Effective leaders embed a common strand of DNA into the life of the congregation. This embedding can happen in several ways from the pastors saying "thus saith the Lord" to a congregational process that might last up to three years. The important thing is that the key leaders of the church, paid and unpaid, all share a common identity.

Resources

- Thomas G. Bandy, *Moving Off the Map* (Nashville: Abingdon Press, 1998)
  Contains a comprehensive congregational model for developing a command strand of DNA and embedding that DNA throughout the congregation.
- Bill Easum, *Unfreezing Moves* (Nashville: Abingdon Press, 2001), pp. 87-94
  Contains a quick method for discovering and articulating the DNA.
- Margaret J. Wheatley, *Leadership and the New Science* (San Francisco: Berrett-Koehler, 1992)
- Richard S. Wellins, William C. Byham, Jeanne M. Wilson, *Empowered Teams* (San Franciso: Jossey-Bass, 1991)

Mission Team Development

Effective leaders know that most of the time spent in a committee is time wasted. Instead, they move the church to a team-based model. The following chart shows the basic difference.

Committee	Team
Committee elected	Individually called
Committee nominated	Leader invites individuals
Standing group that never ends	Is self-ending
Maybe has a mission	Has a clear mission and boundaries
Someone controls final decision	Is autonomous within boundaries
Needs permission to act	Acts on their own within the mission
Not responsible for outcome	Responsible for outcome
Not connected to each other	Connected to each other through DNA

Resources

- Bill Easum and Thomas G. Bandy, *Team Based Ministry* (workbook)
  EBA published, http://www.easumbandy.com, under "Workbooks."
- Thomas G. Bandy, *Coaching Change* (Nashville: Abingdon Press, 2000), pp. 11-127
- Thomas G. Bandy, *Christian Chaos* (Nashville: Abingdon Press, 1999), pp. 179-291
- Wayne Cordeiro, *Doing Church as a Team*, rev. ed. (Ventura: Regal, 2001)
- Richard S. Wellins, William C. Byham, Jeanne M. Wilson, *Empowered Teams* (San Francisco: Jossey-Bass, 1991)

- Patrick Lencioni, *The Five Dysfunctions of a Team: A Leadership Fable* (San Francisco: Jossey-Bass, 2002)

Discernment of Spirit in Culture

The day of the one-church-fits-all is over. Today, effective leaders must be able to read the signs of the times and adjust methodologies to match the culture. Ministry and worship must be indigenous to the area in which the church is located and the people group it wishes to reach. This means that effective leaders function as cultural architects. They know the surrounding community as well as they know their church. They interact with and address the needs of the culture in as many authentic ways as possible.

Resources

- Don Tapscott, *Growing Up Digital* (New York: McGraw-Hill, 1998)
- Lyle E. Schaller, *Discontinuity and Hope: Radical Change and the Path to the Future* (Nashville: Abingdon Press, 1999)
- Stanley Grenz, *A Primer on Postmodernism* (Grand Rapids: Eerdmans, 1996)
- Demographics Web sites: Percept Demographics, www.percept1.com/pacific/start.asp; www.free demographics.com; http://censtats.census.gov/pub/Profiles.shtml
- Matrix Reloaded, http://whatisthematrix.warner-bros.com
- Robert Webber, *The Younger Evangelicals* (Grand Rapids: Baker, 2002)
- J. B. Lightfoot, *The Apostolic Fathers* (Grand Rapids: Baker, 1956)
- Emerging Church, www.emergingchurch.org
- The Gospel and Our Culture Network, www.gocn.org
- The Emergent Friendship, www.emergentvillage.org
- Seven, www.sevenmagazine.org/

Ability to Use Constantly Updateable Technologies

Leaders can no longer rely on the spoken word to do all of the communication of the gospel. Today, many forms of communication are emerging that are far more powerful than the spoken word. To make matters even more dicey, technology is changing so fast that leaders surround themselves with people who are on the cutting edge but just one step away from the bleeding edge of technology (too many bugs are found on the bleeding edge of technology that wise leaders keep close to bleeding edge but not quite on it). Such information is seldom found in traditional book form since by the time a book is published the technology has changed. Instead, leaders look to the Internet and magazines for their information.

Resources

- *Presentations,* VNU eMedia, Minneapolis, Minn., www.presentations.com
- *DV Magazine,* www.dv.com
- *Christian Computing Magazine,* www.ccmag.com

Multiplication of Ministry

Instead of adding members, effective leaders focus on the multiplication of leaders and ministries. They don't just develop a group of leaders; they develop leaders who develop other leaders. They don't just plant churches; they plant churches that plant churches. They don't just form small groups; they form small groups that multiply into more small groups. They don't just mentor one person and release them to do ministry; they mentor several people and release them to go mentor others for ministry. Effective leaders never base their goals on what they can accomplish or what their staff can accomplish or even what their church can accomplish. They are always thinking beyond the boundaries of addition.

Resources

- Bill Easum and Dave Travis, *Beyond the Box* (Loveland, Colo.: Group, 2003)
- Check out the following Web sites that promote multiplication: North Woods Church, www.NorthWood church.org; The Acts 29 Network, www.a29.org; New Heights Church, http://newheights.org; Northwest Church Planting, www.churchplanter.com, Antioch Bible Church, http://www.abchurch.org

Multiplication of Groups

Effective leaders know that more lives are changed in small groups than in large assemblies, so they focus on the multiplication of as many intimate groupings as possible. This requires leaders to think small if they want to reach more people. It also requires leaders to learn the art of multiplication which always results in leaders mentoring and releasing people into leadership positions as soon as possible so that they can go and do the same.

Resources

- M. Scott Boren, *Making Cell Groups Work* (Houston: Cell Group Resources, 2003)
- SmallGroups.com, http://smallgroups.com
- Carl George, *Nine Keys to Effective Small Group Leadership* (Mansfield, Pa.: Kingdom Publishing, 1997)

Mentoring

The transition from teacher to mentor is one of the hardest transitions for leaders, but one that must be done to be an effective leader today. Mentoring is teaching by example. It is on-the-job-training. Mentors have a "to be" list rather than a "to do" list. They are constantly on the lookout for hungry Christians who want to grow in their faith. I remember transitioning from a teacher to mentor. The difference was my goal was no longer to teach a good Bible study but to raise up apprentices from within the group to start other Bible studies.

Resources

- Ken Blanchard, John B. Carlos, and Alan Randolph, *Empowerment Takes More Than a Minute,* 2nd ed. (San Francisco: Berrett-Koehler, 2000)
- Thomas G. Bandy, *Coaching Change* (Nashville: Abingdon Press, 2000), pp. 11-47, 147-79
- Robert Hargrove, *Masterful Coaching* (San Diego: Pfeiffer, 1995)

Community Development

Relationships are replacing place and space as a top issue for leaders. Instead of spending time and income on managing the church property, effective leaders look for ways to transform the community around them and to provide needed basic services in the name of Christ. They take the sanctuary to the streets and allow God's Word to become flesh among non-Christians.

Resources

- Windsor Village United Methodist Church, Houston, TX, www.kingdombuilder.com
- Living Word Christian Center, Forrest Park, Illinois, www.livingwd.org, www.Bwm.org, and www.livingwd.org/kingdom/

City-Reaching Movements

City reaching is somewhat different from community building, although they have similar goals. Community building is usually the project of a single church, as you saw in the resources above. But city reaching is always the result of many churches coming together around a common mission. Instead of attempting to do ministry with other churches through an ecumenical council, often based on similar theologies, effective leaders are partnering with other congregations based on similar missional objectives geared toward inspiring the entire city. These leaders are concerned about getting the churches together around a common mission, not a common table. Mission is the mother of their theology.

Resources

- Jack Dennison, *City Reaching* (Pasadena, Calif.: W. Carey Library, 1999)
- Roger S. Greenway and Timothy M. Monsma, *Cities: Missions' New Frontier*, 2nd ed. (Grand Rapids: Baker, 2000)
- Mission Houston, www.missionhouston.org

Faith Models

Effective leaders do not consider themselves professionals who must develop their leadership. Instead they know they are servants who must model faith in a fishbowl. My partner, Tom Bandy, and I like to speak of the emerging leaders as "spiritual midwives." Their role is helping others birth their God-given gifts. Authentic and effective leaders know that their success in ministry has more to do with whom they mentor and release than what they do themselves.

Resources

- William M. Easum and Thomas G. Bandy, *Growing Spiritual Redwoods* (Nashville: Abingdon Press, 1997)
- Bill Easum, *Leadership on the OtherSide* (Nashville: Abingdon Press, 2000)

Lifestyle Evangelism

Effective leaders know the best form of evangelism is Christians who love one another rather than evangelism programs and committees. Warm, healthy, vibrant, and loving congregations are the best incubators of evangelism and transformation for non-Christians. Effective leaders develop congregations that are so compelling that non-Christians want to be there. The key to evangelism in the New World is the same as it was in the first century—creating environments where people who don't know God can spend time with people who do. This is the primary reason dysfunctional or unfriendly congregations are dying. They just aren't incubators of faith. They repel rather than attract.

Resources

- Brian D. McLaren, *More Ready Than You Realize: Evangelism as Dance in the Postmodern Matrix* (Grand Rapids: Zondervan, 2002)
- Rick Richardson, *Evangelism Outside the Box* (Downers Grove: InterVarsity Press, 2000)
- Michael Green, *Evangelism in the Early Church* (Gainesville, Fla.: Bridge-Logos, 2000)
- Erwin McManus, "Point of View," *Outreach Magazine* (May/June 2003)
- George G. Hunter, *The Celtic Way of Evangelism* (Nashville: Abingdon Press, 2000)

Gift Discernment

Effective leaders provide an environment in which people are encouraged to find and use their God-given gifts instead of being assimilated. In some cases, membership is primarily for leaders. In other cases, membership is eliminated. These leaders soon learn that encouraging people to discern their gifts and put them into ministry means giving up control of what and how ministry happens.

Resources

- Bruce Bugee and Associates Network Ministries International, www.networkministries.com
- Bruce Bugee and Don Cousins, *Network* (Grand Rapids: Zondervan, 1996)
- Bill Easum and Linnea Nilsen Capshaw, *Discovering Our Place in God's World* (workbook) (EBA, 2002), www.easumbandy.com

Congratulations and a Warning

Congratulations. You have finished this part of the journey. Now the real journey begins. Follow your call. Trust your instincts. Listen to the little voice. Develop your skills. But above all, rely on what's percolating within you. Because you can't give what you don't have!

Now I must warn you. The more effective you become, especially in an ineffective congregation, the more trouble will find you and do its best to defeat you. I've never seen any situation that was quite as neat as I've described them in this chapter. Spiritual warfare is one of the most dangerous aspects of leadership in congregations today. That is why you must take care of yourself first. So remember—put on your own oxygen mask first before you try to change your church, much less the world.

It's now time to establish your own personal mission statement if you do not already have one. Even if you do have one, be ready now to reexamine it and see if it really fits your call, preferred style of leadership, context, and your skill set.

CHAPTER TEN

MY PERSONAL MISSION STATEMENT

We're near the end of our journey together. It's time now to develop your own personal mission statement based on all that you've learned and experienced about yourself throughout this book. Developing your own personal mission statement is one of the most important decisions you will ever make in your ministry. Either you will decide the character of your ministry and set your own agenda according to your understanding of God's will for your life, or someone else will decide it for you.

The Relation of Mission Statement to Call

A personal mission statement is like a twin to the call, yet it is different. It comes out of your call; it is an expression of it, and puts feet to your call. It acts as your GPS and keeps you always pointed to the specifics of your call. Your personal mission statement keeps you focused on what is important to carrying out your call. The only time in my ministry I burned out was when I lost sight of that goal. My personal mission statement during all of my ministry has been "equipping every person to be a minister of Jesus Christ."

Consider the following e-mail I received from a trusted friend who is a charter member of our EBA Community:

Subject:	**[advanced-leadership] Re: personal mission statement**
Date:	6/13/2003 10:45:45 PM Central Standard Time
From:	Steve@mindlot.com
Reply to:	advanced-leadership@listsrv.easumbandy.com
To:	advanced-leadership@listsrv.easumbandy.com

My personal mission statement has been a steadying force in my life for about ten years now. It has only changed twice—and not much at that. I developed it during a three-day personal retreat in the mountains of North Georgia. The first time I changed it was after Bill and I went fishing in Kona. Then again after some coaching from Wayne Cordeiro, I added a section that defined my current life phase. I have never found a situation where my personal mission statement didn't help me to get back on track and move forward in my calling. FWIW—Here's mine . . .

Life Verse:

"But by the grace of God I am what I am, and his grace to me was not without effect." 1 Corinthians 15:10

Life Mission:

To fully participate in God's redemption of myself, my family, and my world.

Life Vision:

To serve wholeheartedly in every endeavor in which I participate, forsaking any fear of failure and gratefully accepting challenges as opportunities for service.

Life Values:

Faith: I crave to believe, to change, and to move continually from glory to glory. I'm convinced that fear, uncertainty, and perpetual motion are the hallmarks of a faith-filled life. More than any single quality I desire authenticity. To be so rock-solid convinced that God is who He says He is I can be absolutely honest with my wife, my world, and myself.

Family: God created the family as the vessel through

which people would be taught to follow Him. To create a harmonious, well-functioning team and not create harmony with my wife is unacceptable. To save the world and lose my son is unacceptable. To transform a community and fail to transform my brother is unacceptable.

Legacy: Change has to be lasting to be worthwhile. It is not enough to teach someone what to do, I must teach them why so that they will be able to internalize that change and accept it as their own. If I build an organization into the best it has ever been, but it returns to its previous state upon my departure, then I have wasted their time and failed to genuinely transform it. Success is being replaceable, not essential. This means accepting, and listening, and coaching, and pushing people to take the steps they need in order to be developed into people that accept, and listen, and coach, and push . . .

Discovering daily!

Steve

Time to Do Your Personal Mission Statement

At the beginning of this book, I asked you to keep a log of how you spent your time. If you did, review it to see where your heart burned and your passion was ignited. Those are the places to begin developing your personal mission statement.

Some pastors have one mission statement for their ministry and one for their personal life. Some pastors combine them. Either way is fine. The

Does my day planner reflect what I want to happen in my life?

important thing is that you have a tool that will help keep you and your ministry on course with your call.

Your personal mission statement should be clear enough that the following is true:

- It gives you guidance every step of the way through your life—family, work, and play.
- When you come to the end of your life, you can use it to measure whether or not you feel good about your life.
- Your personal mission statement is short enough for you to easily remember it.

My friend Steve Sjogren graciously submitted the following suggestions for developing a personal mission statement. Steve can be reached at www.stevesjogren.com.

How to Put Together a Life Purpose Statement

by Steve Sjogren

In a recent message at Vineyard Community Church, I made mention of composing a life mission statement. Here are my coaching tips on putting your own purpose statement together.

1. Start with a large sheet of paper. A legal pad will do, but something larger like butcher paper would be even better. Maybe Macaroni Grill® will give you one of their tablecloths!
2. With a bold marker start several lists of words. First begin with words that describe what you have been good at over the years. This can be what others have told you that you are good at. Choose active, descriptive words that capture the imagination. If you are not much of a wordsmith, enlist someone who is gifted in that area. Being precise with words—choosing

words that will move you and others to action and
inspiration—is the objective here.

3. Make your second list words that describe what you
   have enjoyed doing over the years. This could be
   work-related or a discovery you've made related to
   a hobby or with friends or a ministry.

4. Continue a third list with your hobbies and interests. If you are stuck at this point (I sometimes forget the obvious that is right in front of me) get your
   spouse or a good friend to help you list these areas.

5. By now you will probably have several pages of
   notes. Here is where the larger piece of paper or
   butcher paper will come in handy. When I am working with people one-on-one I use large sticky notes—
   these can be purchased at office supply stores. They
   are a great aid in putting together a life purpose statement because not only do they provide the large writing space, but also they have adhesive that allows you
   to stick the entire piece of work on the wall.

6. At this point you are ready to start adding the
   prayer dimension to your process. Of course you
   need to pray and seek God about your purpose. My
   experience is that this sort of thing is revealed in
   prayer over long spans of time through journaling
   more than through a sudden insight in personal
   prayer. On the other hand, if you seek out prophet-
   ic prayer from a gifted person you might receive a
   quick, encouraging insight. At the practical level at
   my church, Vineyard Community Church in Cincin-
   nati, Ohio, you can seek out prayer after one of the
   services or, better yet, you can come to one of the
   special prayer and communion nights that are held
   every couple of months. Call the Vineyard for the
   next scheduled one (513-671-0422).

7. Adding all of these steps together you are ready to
   put together an initial purpose statement. My experience is that you will probably start out with a
   catchall statement that covers all the bases, but is

way too long. My purpose statement was a couple of sentences long at first. I've whittled it down to the essentials of: "Making the dangerous doable."
8. Try out a few versions of your statement on your spouse and friends. This is an exciting adventure you are setting out on. I wish you the best!

It's Time to Rumble

Ministry is beautiful when it is lived out within an authentic call from God. I trust the time we have spent together has helped you get a better handle on that call and what it means to you personally. More important, I trust that our time together will have an impact on the lives of those around you. You have looked into the window of your soul and hopefully have come up enlightened, excited, and focused. Now it's time to leave the comfort of the study or wherever you are and take your faith on the road to mission with Jesus!

Resources

- Laurie Beth Jones, *The Path* (New York: Hyperion, 1996)
- "Focused Living" by Church Resource Ministries, available through Church Smart. It is available in two workbooks, one called *Perspective* and the other *Focus,* or in a weekend retreat format.
- Tom and Christine Sine, *Living on Purpose: Finding God's Best for Your Life* (Grand Rapids: Baker, 2002)
- John Schuster, *Answering Your Call: A Guide for Living Your Deepest Purpose* (San Francisco: Berrett-Koehler, 2003)
- Thomas G. Bandy, *Moving Off the Map* (Nashville: Abingdon Press, 1998)
- J. Robert Clinton, *The Making of a Leade*r (Colorado Springs, Colo.: NavPress, 1988)

SECTION 4
APPENDIXES

APPENDIX 1

MY JOURNAL

Many forms of journalizing are in vogue today. If you have a favorite method, use it. If you aren't accustomed to journalizing, you may want to use this one. Whatever you do, consistency is important. Consider writing thirty minutes to an hour each day.

A Suggested Form of Journalizing

Allow the following questions to be the backdrop for your journal. Refer to them each time you make an entry. Let them become your *Shema*.

- Will my legacy be a "who" or a "what"? Am I going to equip and empower people or manage an institution?
- Which occupies most of my time—caring for people or transforming them?
- Am I still in touch with my call and is it still directing my life?
- Is my call big enough and worthy enough to die for? If not, why?
- How deep is my passion for Jesus Christ? Have I literally wept over the fact that so many around me never experience God through Christ?

125

- How solid is my personal relationship with Jesus Christ?
- What do I do regularly to nurture my soul?

As you write in your journal, make note of:

- Favorite Scriptures that pop into your mind.
- Experiences you've had in the past that were extra meaningful to you and gave direction to your life.
- Friends and mentors along the way that have had a significant impact on your life. Over time, send them a note telling them how much they have meant to your spiritual journey.
- "Aha!" moments—those times when everything seems to make perfect sense.
- Directions from God that you know you must follow.
- Thoughts that you should share with fellow travelers.

126

APPENDIX 2

OPPORTUNITIES FOR WITHDRAWAL

Here is a list of opportunities for withdrawal times. I'm sure you can add to this list. The key is to find the method that appeals to your personality.

- Go on a two-day overnight retreat by yourself. Some of the most important things in life happen during our dreams. Many of the prophets received their visions while asleep. Don't overestimate the connection between deep contemplation, deep sleep, and God's vision. Take only your Bible and a blank legal pad. It may surprise you to know that God usually has an agenda. Do not take any "to do" stuff. There is nothing you need to do on this retreat other than listen to God. If it has been awhile since you have done this, you may need to add a third day or do it more than once before you are satisfied with the results.
- Keep a daily journal. Review it now and then to see where you're making progress and where you struggle the most and to remind you of why you began the journey.
- Commune with nature. One of my joys in life is to be fifty or sixty miles out in the ocean and watch the sun come up. The experience always reminds me of God's glory and of my insignificant role.

- Join a health club with your spouse and schedule a time for the two of you to go. What is good for the body is usually good for the soul.
- Begin each day at home with prayer and train folks at the church not to expect you in the office until 10:00 or even later. Do not check your e-mail before going to the office.
- Develop a habit of praying an hour or so each morning before tackling the day.
- Plan a yearly vacation and take it no matter what.
- Find a spiritual director. This is a trained person who listens and guides another person in deepening their walk with God, discerning God's will for their life, and praying for that person. The goal of this relationship is obedience to God's call. It is not counseling, but clearly based in listening, discerning, and following God's Word at a certain time and place in a person's journey. Many denominations have a section on their Web page for spiritual directors.
- Develop an accountability group. This is a group of people that you trust to objectively give you feedback on your ministry. Meet with them regularly. Ask them to hold you accountable to what you are called to do. Perhaps give them a two-by-four with your name written on it. If you're like me, sometimes you're so headstrong that you remind yourself and others of the proverbial mule.
- Do some form of meditation and don't overlook such things as tai chi or yoga. God can use most forms of meditation to the kingdom's advantage.
- Ask a group in the church to pray for you. Studies show that people in hospitals who are prayed for do better even when they do not know people are praying for them.
- Talk with the leaders of your church about customizing your time off to suit your personality.

Some high-charging people need more than one day off a week to recharge. If you are not a one-day-off-a-week person, take regular time away from ministry. Every four weeks or so, my wife and I would get lost for four or five days. We went to the beach. This worked for us better than a day off each week.

• Read about the spiritual giants of the past and present. I've found great inspiration reading about Rosa Parks, Nelson Mandela, Gandhi, and Bonhoeffer. Who are the great spiritual giants in your life? Reflect on them.

• Listen to your favorite music. The younger a person is today, the more likely music will be a major form of renewal of the soul. My spirit soars when I hear music like "My Prayer," "Majesty," "God of Grace and God of Glory," and believe it or not, "I'll Fly Away." What music fills your soul and turns you on to the wonder around you?

APPENDIX 3

ALTERNATIVE CAREERS FOR
TODAY'S DISTRESSED CLERGY

---

by Edward Hammett

As a seminary-trained professional involved in denominational, seminary, and local church life, I've encountered, within myself at times and in other colleagues, a sense of unrest, unease, and distress with our career—not necessarily our calling. Because I travel in and out of many churches and seminary classrooms I'm encountering more and more of my peers who "want out of ministry," "feel trapped in their career," or who are wondering "what other careers does my ministry degree equip me for?" Still others indicate the exhausting frustration with their churches and denominations because of the infighting over political and superficial issues that mean nothing to carrying out the Great Commission or the Great Commandment. Others tell me that if they don't leave the church they'll lose their family, for their churches expect them to be at every meeting, every surgery, every funeral (and there's a growing number of these in most of our churches) and to be proficient to counsel the ever-growing complexity of family and personal problems.

So what are distressed pastors to do? If they're realizing that for their sake, the sake of their families, and the sake of the ministry they need to either take a break from the local congregation or consider another career that fulfills the calling, what should they do?

What career alternatives are out there for this growing host of disillusioned, disenfranchised, and distressed clergy? How can a committed and called person find fulfillment and integrity in other careers and remain true to the calling to ministry? I think there's great hope and many opportunities emerging. This article will simply try to summarize the emerging opportunities I'm encountering.

Understanding the Distress of Today's Clergy

Today's clergy face what seem to be insurmountable mountains of challenges on just about every front of their career and calling. Permit me to simply provide a working list of challenges:

- Most were trained in seminary for a world and a church that no longer exist. Seminaries seemed determined to preserve classical European models effective in a churched culture, while the culture has shifted and the local church needs have shifted. Some seminaries are making needed curriculum changes with high degrees of success. But for some seminaries, we have miles to go before an effective model is found that will produce new leaders.
- Most congregations' leadership cores and tithing cores are aging out. These changes create many challenges and opportunities that are calling on skill sets and faith formation that many clergy lack and many congregations aren't ready for or open to pursuing.

- Spiritual leadership, oddly enough, is something that hasn't often been effectively modeled or taught, and therefore we have some clergy slipping into CEO mentalities and models.
- Church polity is outdated in many ways for our secular culture challenges. Decision making is laborious at best in most traditions, and younger people aren't going to be stuck in this cycle of getting permission while the older generation feels this is the "way we do things around here."
- Generational differences are pressing on every front. Worship wars are everywhere because various age groups prefer different styles. Curriculum battles are present for similar reasons. Time frame and program offerings face similar challenges. Blending services often leads to congregational confusion and creates an unhappy exodus or tension-filled church life.
- Pastors' families are facing challenges every other family seems to be facing these days. Divorce, remarriage, challenges with children and teenagers, communication battles, dealing with family-of-origin issues, dysfunctions, and the stresses related to living in a "fish bowl."
- Compassion fatigue is epidemic among clergy who are expected to do all the pastoral care themselves. How many times have you as a pastor been called back from family vacations for funerals, emergencies, and often called away from your own family to care for other families?
- Continuing education opportunities are rampant, but many church leaders and members don't see the need for their pastors to go away two or three times a year for such relevant training. If they "allow them to go" (rather than encourage or expect them to go), they often restrict how much the church will pay for the expenses that might be incurred. Yet the reality is that continuing education is a necessity—not an option.

133

While this list is only suggestive, it shows us the challenges we face and that seem to be contributing to the growing distress. Such issues and challenges are creating a growing leadership crisis in many churches today.

Leadership Crisis in Christendom

The intense and pervasive challenges in our church and culture are creating a leadership crisis in many churches and denominations. Several valuable studies have been done the last several years that document this crisis in much better ways than I'll summarize here. If you want to do further study, see research and resources on the following Web sites:

- www.alban.org
- www.alban.org/pdf/leadership.pdf
- http://hirr.hartsem.edu/research/research_con-gregtnl_studies.html
- www.clergyrenewal.org

These sites will provide statistical data and hard data that explains the crisis pastors are facing in ministry today. I want to share with you some observations and soft data that will put a face to this epidemic among our clergy.

Some of our best and brightest are leaving church ministry for secular careers. Last year, on my personal calendar, I started listing the pastors from my connections in the southeast United States who notified me they were leaving the church for a secular career. I had at least four names every week listed on my calendar for the entire year.

Let me share with you some excerpts from an e-mail I received this week from a colleague contemplating a career move and struggling with his dissatisfaction:

"As you note in your writing, I'm a pastor who spends much of my time (especially in a retirement community like this) holding hands with folks who expect the pastor to hold hands with them but who do not need the pastor to hold hands with them. I am very much, in Carlyle Marney's words, 'a kept harlot.' I work way too many hours a week, and I spend those hours with people that Jesus would not have invested so much time with. And I can't go to my supervisor and ask to block out time to build relationships with unchurched people. I could go to the deacons and my deacons would be supportive. But when the phone rings and somebody who knows the Lord wants me to go see somebody else who knows the Lord, I'm still expected to go. If I say, 'Sorry, but I really wanted to go hang with some lost people,' I would be out of a job soon enough.

"I have three kids. One is about to start college. The other two will start college soon enough. I need a job that pays. My salary package is actually pretty generous, and I am thankful for that. The people like me and they are supportive of me. Yet what we are doing is not all of what we need to be doing. Indeed, it is my conviction that the most important part of our calling goes largely undone, and that calling is to build bridges to the people like you have been building bridges toward."

Ministerial burnout is rampant. I know a number of colleagues who are on mood altering medications in order to get help with depression, stress, and mood swings. Other indicators of this are those ministers fighting with sexual temptations, pornography, family pressures, and low self-image and self-esteem.

Two good resources for dealing with ministerial burnout are *Beating Burnout* (Alban Institute) by Lynne Baab (www.alban.org) and *Crash Without Burning* (Smyth & Helwys) by David Matthew (www.helwys.com).

Financial stress and complications. Several colleagues are facing retirement or are currently in retirement with no home (because they have lived in parsonages) and little or no retirement funds because their churches have provided little or no retirement plans and insufficient salaries. Those still working are stressed because their children are moving into college and they have no funds or savings.

Many churches aren't able or choose not to provide sufficient salary packages. Research does indicate this is improving in some areas of the country and within several denominations. However, this financial crunch is a major reason some pastors are leaving the church—today's economy just requires more to live than it used to. The amount of education of many clergy and the amount of their salaries are out of line with other comparable degrees and professions.

These and many other elements are involved in the leadership crises being faced among out churches today. In many parts of the country, there aren't enough pastors and priests to go around. More churches and fewer priests and pastors create a paralyzing vacuum. In some places this vacuum is forcing the lay leaders to step up to the plate and pick up some of the responsibilities that Scripture says belong to them—but they had relegated to clergy for decades.

One pastor friend was seriously ill for months—and his formerly pastor-dependent church cared for him, supported him through various surgeries and recoveries, picked up the slack, and performed responsibilities of ministry very efficiently and effectively. When he recovered and was back in the saddle again, they handed it all back to him. He refused to take it and then affirmed them and validated their ministry and effectiveness. He suggested that was the way the New Testament church was to function. They refused to continue their ministry and fired him.

Alternative Careers for Today's Clergy

As we can see, ministry often seems overwhelming and fruitless for the amount of effort one expends, and it seems impossible to meet the mounting and often unrealistic expectations by church members who would prefer to keep things the way they are than change things in order to reach others. Such realities are prompting many pastors to explore alternative careers. Below are listings of those options I've noted as I've listened to the disenchanted and walked with some of them through this maze of calling and ministry options. Certainly this isn't an exhaustive list but indicative. Many pastors seeking alternative careers often have a difficult time translating their multiple ministry skills into new careers and new résumés.

Faith-based organizations—offer many opportunities for clergy that often are a win-win for everyone. The pastor's looking to continue his or her calling, and the faith-based organization needs a person of faith with team-building, fund-raising, and management skills to move them forward. The Peter F. Drucker Foundation offers much guidance these days to FBOs and those in their employment. The current government administration is working very hard to create more FBOs and is investing more time and money into their creation.

Nonprofit organizations—also offer many opportunities. While many FBOs are nonprofit, there are other nonprofit organizations that aren't FBOs. Working through local business organizations or the chamber of commerce may open the door of opportunity.

Social service agencies—are great matches for people who want to help others. The helping professions are varied and the government offices are always looking for people to help with protective services, counseling, financial counseling, adoption issues, food services, and financial support services.

Teaching profession—in public and private schools. Higher education, home schooling, and classrooms for people of all ages need teachers, and a minister's skills often translate beautifully. Sometimes further training is needed for certification.

Management and human resources—are other naturals

for those clergy who are appropriately gifted. Businesses of all types are looking for those who manage finances, personnel, resources, and community relations. (www.astd.org)

Writing—captures the hearts of many pastors. Sermon writing and delivery is great training for that first novel, Christian books, management books, or those words that simply share your story. Attend a writer's conference and see what happens!

Consulting—is natural for some. Take the lessons you've learned in the school of hard knocks and create a business forum with others who can help lead churches and leaders forward in faith and function. There's a growing demand and respect for these entrepreneurs across all denominational lines. (www.coaching.com, www.internal-impact.com)

Coaching—is a growing field and holds much promise for fulfilling the Great Commission and the Great Commandment in many fields of life. We're told that coaching will have a strong future in areas of spiritual-life coaches, career coaches, food coaches, parenting coaches, marriage coaches, and many other arenas. (www.coaching.com, www.christiancoachesnetwork.com, www.hollifield.org, www. leadingideas.org)

Financial management/fund-raising—is another natural for some. Managing budgets, raising funds, and creating multiple funding streams for ministry is great training for many financial careers. Financial planning, financial resourcing, banking, fund-raising, and financial oversight for conventions or businesses are just a few places to serve.

Funeral home industry—is another natural. Death is inevitable and many unchurched people need care and support during this time. Bereavement counseling and creation of support services and partnerships with churches for helping people are critical and valuable ministries.

Organizational management—is a career for the administratively gifted. Businesses of all kinds are looking for help in this area in an age of downsizing and retooling of organizations. (www.astd.org)

Research and resource development—are avenues of ministry that many explore and find great satisfaction. Many philanthropists are willing to fund entrepreneurial research and development projects through grants and foundation gifts. (www.fdncenter.org)

Media and Web-based learning—is for those who have passions for television, radio, media, and Web-based learning and design.

Marketing—has become a skill of many clergy that the business world can benefit from and accommodate.

Government/politics—are avenues where the world needs people of faith and integrity. Run for an office in your community, county, state, or nation. Follow your passions and callings in the world.

Pastor in the business world—where many Fortune 500 companies and businesses across the world are hiring pastors to care for their employees and to rebuild trust and integrity in the community in which they serve. (www.hischurchatwork.org, www.avodahinstitute.org, www.marketplaceministry.org, www.icwm.net, www.marketplaceministries.com, www.ninetyandnine.com, www.transformingsolutions.org) *The Soul of the Firm* (Zondervan) by C. William Pollard, and *The Gathered and Scattered Church* (Smyth & Helwys) by Edward Hammett.

Coaching Helps in Transitions

Some research has been done indicating that about 55 percent of today's pastors are transitioning locations of ministry each year. The research is also clear that those pastors who stay in ministry in the midst of distress are able to do so because they have a coach/mentor in ministry. Those making career transitions, life transitions, location transitions, or other types of ministry transitions are much happier if they're coached through the transition. I'd encourage those facing such transitions or distress to consider hiring a coach. Coaching sessions are all about you, about your agendas, and a confidential and trusting relationship with someone. The coach has your best interests at heart and is trained to ask questions to help you discover the best answers for you, to help you avoid blind spots, and to align your decisions with discernment of God's call. Coaches can be found in many places. You might want to interview several coaches before making your selections. Christian coaches can be discovered by visiting www.christiancoachesnetwork.com, www.hollifield.org, www.coaching.com, or other sites can be found on the link page of www.transformingsolutions.org.

It's my hope that this article might stimulate a conversation among church leaders, denominational executives, and business leaders and provide some encouragement and hope for those distressed. I'm convinced that God's doing a new work among his people and is scattering many of his best and brightest into the workplace in daily life to be salt, light, and leaven in the world.

I hope this article will stimulate dialogues online and in learning communities of searching persons. If you want to dialogue more about this article, join my online community. If you're interested visit www.transformingsolutions.org.

Edward Hammett is a congregational and personal coach with the Baptist State Convention of North Carolina. His most current book is *Reframing Spiritual Formation: Discipleship in an Unchurched Culture* (Smyth & Helwys). (www.transformingsolutions.org)

TRANSLATING MINISTRY SKILLS INTO ALTERNATIVE PROFESSIONS (PATHWAYS OF TRANSITION FOR DISTRESSED CLERGY)

by *Edward Hammett*

My previous article, "Alternative Careers for Today's Distressed Clergy," reviews the reasons some clergy are exploring leaving the local church ministry for alternative careers as well as overviews some of the alternative professions being explored and embraced by an increasing number of clergy. This article will summarize some of the pathways found to be effective in translating skills from local church ministry into alternative careers. It is my hope that the article can provide some coaching to help those seeking discernment about alternative professions and venues of ministry.

While some would suggest that the exodus of clergy from local church professions represents their inadequacy or unfaithfulness, I believe that many of the clergy shifting professions is simply another manifestation of their initial calling into ministry. In today's increasingly secular world where fewer and fewer people are attracted to or involved in local churches, there's an increasing number of opportunities to minister to persons through the workplace. What if God is putting some of his best and brightest ordained and unordained clergy in positions to reach and minister to the unchurched seven days a week in their vocations? What are the ministry skills used in local church ministry that can be translated into résumés that will help ensure movement into alternative professions?

Helping Clergy Find Their Place in New Professions

Call, giftedness, and a sense of "sent-ness" are still at the core of discerning God's movement and placement in life and career. The following questions might help clarify one's call, giftedness, and "sent-ness" into ministry in and through a secular career.

- To what profession are you attracted, pulled?
- For which careers do you find you have a long-standing appreciation?
- What persons do you respect and value for the things they do in their work life?
- What energizes you? What are the careers and places this energy can be channeled into with ease?
- What do you have a high motivation to do?
- In what areas of life do you get the most results and satisfaction?
- What areas of local church ministry did you enjoy the most and find the most fulfillment in doing?
- What arenas of local church ministry did you least enjoy and avoid when possible?

Just because some clergy are no longer finding fulfillment in their current ministry doesn't mean that God can't use them in significant ways, for kingdom purposes, by planting them in new careers and professions that can be effective avenues of ministry. After all there are many illustrations in Scripture of persons in careers outside the church walls that had significant impact on the kingdom. What about Nehemiah, a great manager who helped persons have a "mind to work" and rebuild the temple? Moses was used significantly as a keeper of Jethro's sheep. David was a savy politician that God used greatly. Then there were those physicians, teachers, fishermen, tax collectors, farmers, and business owners that God used mightily in his kingdom's work in the New Testament narratives. So ministry through secular careers is not an unknown in God's plan and purpose. (*Word in Life Study Bible* is a great resource to track them as well as *The Marketplace Annotated Bibliography* by Pete Hammond or www.workplaceministry.org.)

Coaching Clergy Forward into a New Profession

What will help clergy seeking new professions move forward into a new profession? These are steps many have found helpful:

1. Enlist a coach that can help move you forward, restore confidence in your skill set and competencies, as well as pray with you about God's leading into a new profession.
2. Create a résumé built on strengths recognized and affirmed in local church ministry that can easily be translated into new professions.
3. Translate ministry and academic accomplishments into a résumé for a secular career.

4. Create a support system for the displaced clergy while seeking new placement.
5. Create an action plan for moving into your new profession and creating an accountability group for fulfilling your calling in the new career.
6. Last but not least pray for the transition and discernment of God's leading into a new mission field and ministry opportunity.

Enlist a Coach

Sometimes we are so close to something that we need an objective eye, ear, or voice. Very often this is true while trying to reinvent yourself and your résumé. Enlisting a certified professional coach can be money well spent in the business of reinventing yourself and clarifying a new calling and new profession. There are several places you can find this coach. Christian Coaches Network (www.christian-coachesnetwork.com) is a starting place. Then there's transforming leadership (www.transformationalcoaching.com), then searching on the Web will avail you of many possibilities. Usually the first interview is by phone and usually free to see if there is chemistry and compatibility. My Web site and others will offer you many links you will want to explore.

A coach offers companionship for the journey and a network of persons in various careers that can help in placement and encouragement. A coach asks questions—similar to the questions I'm framing in this article. A coach also offers encouragement and accountability for moving forward rather than for moving in circles.

Create a Résumé Built on Strengths

Local church ministry is more often than not very complex and calls on a vast array of skills—some we are good at and some we are not. When building this new résumé think of your strengths—explore this with your coach and ask others you have been leading to assess your strengths and weaknesses. Do a mental inventory. List on paper those strengths you have exercised through the years. Prioritize this list as to those strengths you are energized by and those that usually produce fruit. Now take these strengths and list them on a résumé as your working skill set and areas of competency. The following list might get you started:

- People skills—working with gifted persons, working with difficult people, working in small groups, working with large groups
- Conflict management
- Managing change
- Managing personnel
- Computer skills
- Curricula design
- Public speaking
- Community resource
- Financial management
- Crises and personal growth counseling
- Caregiving
- Mentoring and coaching
- Leadership development
- Organizational development
- Building management
- Partnership building

See, the list is not difficult to come up with nor are the areas of strength difficult to translate into the secular job market. There are many resources that can help in this process. The following are possible starting places: *What Color Is Your Parachute?* by Boles; Po Bronson's *What Should I Do With My Life?*; www.pobronson.com; www.strengthsquests.com; www.crown.org; www.workplaceministry.org.

Translate Ministry and Academic Accomplishments

What are the academic and ministry accomplishments you have enjoyed? How might these accomplishments be framed on a new résumé targeting a new profession? This is often challenging, difficult, and discouraging at first glance. I've heard many clergypersons say, "What else does my training prepare me to do? I'm trapped in ministry. No other employer wants a divinity degree in his staff."

While this may be your impression, today's marketplace is more open to such degrees and training than ever before. Because of the Enron scandals and other failures of integrity in the business world, many businesses are looking for persons to raise the level of integrity of their staff and the public perception of their company. In fact, a prominent pastor in Atlanta just recently moved into the SunBank Corporation as the Officer of Community Conscience. What a great ministry and opportunity!

Now let's explore some ministry skills and academic achievements that might launch you into a new profession. Consider:

- Number of new clients (members) you have attracted and reached
- Number of staff you have successfully supervised and helped grow forward into their career
- Number of volunteers your have enlisted, supervised, and watched reach their potential and grow forward
- Programs you have designed, staffed, implemented, and evaluated
- Financial base you have raised, managed, and secured
- Relationships you have managed and matured to accomplish assigned tasks
- Persons you have helped place in positions that maximize their potential and giftedness

• Impact of your public speaking at challenging, changing, and transforming persons into leaders and more faithful and effective persons

See, once again, it's really not that overwhelming. You just have to think a little differently. Your skill set is solid.

What about academic achievements? Many have Masters or Doctor of Ministry degrees. How does this translate? Give yourself credit for the discipline of graduate or post-graduate studies, continuing education, and all the reading you have done through the years. List your areas of proficiency, passion, and participation: for example, history, management, curricula design, organizational development, finances, business management, personnel, business ethics, community or public relations.

Create a Support System

Support is essential in this life transition. Support of family is vital, but most need for time with family to be family time and not always time supporting you in life and career change. Enlist a support group of peers who might be going through or contemplating something similar. Contact persons at your state or regional judicatory or denominational office and ask if they know of others in similar circumstances, maybe an on-line forum with persons across the country. (You will note that I often use an on-line forum—visit www.transformingsolutions.org for more information.) Sometimes there are community groups facilitated by a career counselor. Watch the local newspapers. Also there are many career ministries being hosted by local churches to help persons reinvent themselves during these tough economic times in which many are being downsized and are retooling for new careers.

Talk with your pastor, peers, and friends to find the support and encouragement to keep you moving forward. Your coach will be a certain and stable source of support and may be a network to others.

Create an Action Plan and Accountability

Again, when the tides of life seem to be changing and life becomes stressed and in somewhat of a whirlwind, often we go in circles out of panic rather than intentionally moving forward. A coach helps move you forward. Support groups help move you forward and hold you accountable for finding and taking the next steps toward a new career. An action plan might include: answering questions raised in this article, translating and fashioning a new résumé, finding the new career possibilities and doing some preliminary research on the Web or by interview about the company or opportunity. What about reading, working through some of the inventories on the web I've mentioned? What about the challenge of making two or three contacts per day? Post your new résumé on several of the Internet job search sites. Working your network from peer relationships, and present and past church relationships. Maybe you can ask some others to review and adjust your new résumé. What about attending a career counseling session offered in your community? Finding a new job becomes your job if you are no longer in a full-time position. If you are in a job while looking for a new career then this research becomes your avocation.

Pray for Guidance, Strength, and Discernment

Prayer is last but is certainly not the least important. Praying for guidance, discernment, and strength are vital. Establish time and place to pray about new career possibilities. Enlist a prayer partner to share this time with you.

Discerning God's leadership is vital to ensure that you are found serving and ministering in the place he is calling you to serve in. Such will certainly allow you to feel good about yourself to ensure that you are continuing to follow God's call upon your life—just in a different venue.

As you work on the résumé, build a new support base and accountability relationships. Look for places and people that are consistent with your calling. Be aware of places and issues that prove to be a disconnect with your passions, purpose, calling. Look for dialogues and opportunities that are landmarks in your pilgrimage that parallel your calling and gifting rather than walking into landmines that don't seem to meet your skill set or calling.

Be patient with yourself and with God. Remember he calls and sends people into the church and as the church into the world to be his presence and representative there. In times like we live, the ministry of the people of God in the world is as critically important as the ministry of the local church. Go forth and learn to be salt, light, and leaven in the world and to "reap the harvest" while it is still in the fields. We need your ministry and the knowledge you will encounter in your new mission field.

APPENDIX 4

FAITH AT WORK
GUIDELINES FOR GROUPS

1. Engage yourself in the process. Don't just observe. Let Christ center the group.
2. Tell your own story. Emphasize experience over analysis.
3. Listen with your heart. Receive feelings and facts as given. Judge not.
4. Model by doing. Be vulnerable, open, affirming.
5. Give no advice!
6. Share time equally.
7. The right to pass.
8. Practice confidentiality. Keep stories contained in the group.
9. Exercise your power to bless! Call forth one another's gifts.
10. Be accountable for your own growth.
11. We care; Christ cures. Pray for one another.

Faith@Work, Fall Church, Virginia, www.FaithAt-Work.com

CHANGING YOUR ENABLER STYLE

Y ou can change your enabling style if you want to. This section is for you if you have a burning desire to be a transformational leader but one or more of the following is getting in your way:

- You choose statement two on page 76.
- Your preferred style is enabler.
- Your mercy gift makes it hard for you to lead.

Discerning the Issue

The first thing you must discern is whether your condition is a strength or weakness. One of the paradoxes of life is that our greatest strengths are also our greatest weaknesses. There's a thin line between gift and addiction. Take the gift of mercy, for example. It is definitely a gift from God. However, when it becomes an obstacle to doing what God wants done, it's possible the gift has become an addiction. Instead of adding strength to our character, it weakens us. For example: some of your desire to take care of people may not be driven by an authentic mercy gift, but rather is rooted in old issues of self-esteem, conflict avoidance, or merely needing people to like you because you never felt liked when growing up. Your actions may appear to be driven by mercy when in fact they are driven by an inner weakness. So, before working on compensating for a mercy gift by developing a strength, focus on strengthening what is weak. If you do decide your enabler style is a weakness more than a gift, get counseling to help you with whatever might be in your background that lowers your self-esteem and ego.

But there is another possible reason for your actions, other than having a high mercy gift. Your inability to lead could be because you have succumbed to the pressure from your peers to conform to an understanding of the role of the pastor that is not biblical. You know your present style of leadership is really not your preferred style. You are just doing what everyone else says you ought to do. If that describes you, then forget what everyone is telling you and start following your call. You will have some relearning to do since you have buried your natural inclinations. I know, because I almost lost my way listening to my peers.

Overcoming a High Mercy Gift

However, if you are confident that neither of the above two options apply to you and that your inability to lead is due to a high mercy gift, please know you still can be a leader if you want to badly enough.

Here are two e-mails I received from clients who successfully dealt with their mercy gift:

Subject:	**Re: overcoming mercy addiction**
Date:	6/13/2003 1:04:16 PM Central Standard Time
From:	Jimmy@xfamc.com
To:	Easum@aol.com

Bill and others,
I was a mercy addict. The only way I was able to overcome that addiction was absolute surrender to

Jesus. I didn't overcome it, really. Jesus is stronger than my addiction to being merciful. Whether it tweaked my inside or not, I said no to giving in or feeling sorry for anyone who did not get it. I prayed and prayed and listened and journaled, becoming very deeply aware of the addiction to pleasing people, to making them feel good about themselves instead of helping them to face reality.

Life is too short to be focused on the few whiners who expect mercy. There is a world desperately in need of what Jesus has to offer and there is nothing that I won't give up (all right at least that I have discovered yet—I'll have to submit that to Jesus when I discover it). Jesus helped me to decide there was nothing anyone could take from me that held power enough to make me be merciful enough to let things that mattered slide.

Mercy rears its ugly head periodically when I least expect it. All I can do then is admit my powerlessness over it and give it to Jesus again. He is big enough to handle it and anything else I need help with.

Give up on mercy before it kills you or stops you from becoming part of Jesus' mission movement in the world.

Subject:	**[advanced-leadership] Re: Easum**
Date:	6/16/2003 10:54:29 AM Central Standard Time
From:	rhsc@mindsprung.com
Reply to:	advanced-leadership@listsrv.easumbandy.com
To:	advanced-leadership@listsrv.easumbandy.com

Bill,

For me, it took 6 years out of the pastorate. Working a real job in the real world and having 80+ employees to hold accountable taught me a lot I never learned in the pastorate. While pastoring and having high mercy gifts, I too easily fell prey to the prevailing notion among church members that my job was to keep them all happy. So that's what I tried to do . . . without much success I might add.

After leaving the pastorate and becoming the director of a children's home, I learned that we had a very clear mission as an agency/organization. The treatment and welfare of approximately 80 at-risk teenagers was primary, not the happiness quotient of the employees. I learned to fire anyone who wasn't on board with the mission of the children's home. It became easy after a while, because I was clear on why we were in existence.

Upon my return to the pastorate (kicking and screaming all the way—I thought I had escaped, and didn't want to go back), I approached it with the same mission-driven approach I had learned at the children's home. Once you answer the "why are we here?" question, the rest starts to fall into place. I was no longer concerned with keeping people happy, only keeping us in the mission. Folks who aren't on board are invited to leave. I understand now that it's not being hard-hearted; it's being mission-focused.

I'm not sure I could have ever overcome the high mercy gifts if I had remained in the church culture. So, it may take getting out into the real world, out of the anemic culture that is found in many churches, to get some of us back to Christ's mission.

Thanks for asking.

Jim

If you want to redirect your high mercy gift, I suggest:

- Continually pray that God will give you the strength to do the hard things you don't want to do. God can change us at our deepest level if we allow it to happen.
- Make sure that you have at least one close, competent person on your team who has very low mercy gifts. You know, a hit person. Watch how this person

addresses painful issues and learn.

- Spend time coaching yourself to do the hard things as often as you can, like supervision, or stopping someone when they are speaking out against someone else, or disrupting a board meeting.
- Coaching should come naturally to an authentic mercy gift, so use that skill a lot.

> Hi, my name is Bill and I'm merciful. I'm powerless to change it on my own. But one day at a time, I will rely on Jesus Christ to make me the kind of person who can not only care for people, but also be an instrument of change in their lives.

- Spend time around entrepreneurial pastors and churches. This will help you get over the dysfunctions that might be in the background, like church or family.
- Constantly remind yourself that you want to change lives. Don't let your mercy gift become an addiction. Confess it to someone and ask them to pray for you.
- Above all, revisit your call every day and bask in the wonder of it until it consumes you once again.

Resources

- 12 Steps of Recovery, http://www.12step.org/, using *The Serenity Bible.* You may even want to attend weekly recovery meetings.
- Edwin Friedman, *A Failure of Nerve: Leadership in the Age of the Quick Fix* (Bethesda, Md.: Edwin Friedman Estate/Trust, 1999)
- Larry Matthews's program in Lost River, West Virgina, which grew out of Friedman's center, http://www.leadershipinministry.com
- Larry Foster's year-long program, http://www.clergy-seminars.net

THE PROBLEM WITH MERCY GIFTS

I've seen a disturbing pattern throughout my consulting ministry: most established churches are held hostage by one or two bullies. One individual or small group of individuals are usually extremely opposed to the church making any radical change, even if it means the change would give the church a chance to thrive once again. I keep hearing pastors say, "If I tried that, I'd lose my job!"

Courageous pastors often ask, "What do I do when one person intimidates the church so much that it is not willing to try something new?" My response is always, "Either convert them, neutralize them, or ask them to leave. The Body cannot live with cancer." To which someone usually cries, "That's not very Christian!" These folks just don't understand the seriousness of hampering the Body of Christ.

My response describes much of the wisdom of both the Old Testament and Jesus. Maturing Christians love so deeply that they will do anything, even not being nice, for the sake of the gospel. Jesus was so compassionate toward others that he could not remain quiet when he saw people holding other people in bondage.

The Old Testament story of the wilderness wanderings contains a remarkable account of how Moses responded to a group of people who insisted on keeping the Hebrews' bondage to the past (Numbers 16). A group of people led by Korah came to Moses asking him to relinquish leadership because they wanted to take the Hebrews back to Egypt. Moses responded by falling on his face prostrate before them in prayer. Then he got up and slew all of them. Not very nice, but necessary if they were going to get to Canaan. Moses knew that freedom with God was better than slavery with Pharaoh. The same is true today: freedom to grow in grace is always better than enslavement to the status quo.

Almost every struggling church has at least one dysfunctional bully who goes out of his or her way to be a big fish in a small pond. Often that is the primary reason the church is struggling. This person gets his or her sense of self-worth by keeping the church so intimidated, either by his or her actions or his or her money, that very little can happen without that person's approval. The sad thing is that most of the leaders know that this person is a stumbling block to the church's future and they will not do anything about it. The church leaders ignore the bully, thinking that is the Christian thing to do, and in so doing, assist in the stunted growth or death of the congregation.

For example, I was working with a staff in a large church. The first day I met with the staff the tension was so high I could cut the air with a knife. The staff hardly said a word to one another. The next day when we met the staff laughed and cut up together as if they were one big happy family. As I looked around the table, the only apparent difference was that one staff person was not present. I asked the staff if they sensed the difference I was feeling. They knew exactly what I meant. Finally one of them blurted out, "Jim is not here today. Staff meetings are always better when he's not here." It turned out that Jim was a dysfunctional bully who ran to the personnel committee every time he didn't get his way. Because of him, several competent staff members had been fired. To make matters worse, the staff knew that Jim seldom contributed anything to the health and vitality of the church.

I asked the staff if they had confronted Jim with how they felt. Their response was typical for church folks. "That would not be the Christian thing to do. It would hurt him deeply. After all, the church is all he has." Sure, it's all that he has; no one else would put up with him. Who is more dysfunctional, Jim or the staff?

A church not far from me put out the word that it wanted a young pastor. It wasn't long before they got one. One of the first things the young pastor did was ask the board to change the appearance of the church newspaper. The board unanimously voted to do so. Four months later, I noticed the newspaper was switched back to its old form. I called the pastor to ask why. His response is a classic. "Most of the board were present the night we voted. However, one man was out of the country. When he returned to find that a decision had been made in his absence, he demanded that the chairperson immediately call another meeting. At the second meeting, the board voted unanimously to rescind their previous decision about the newspaper." When I asked why, he replied: "This man always pays off any deficit at the end of year and he wanted the vote changed. The board was afraid to buck him." The future of that church was held hostage by a bully.

One of the main sins of the established church is that we have taught ourselves to be nice instead of to be Christian. In spite of aspiring to be a disciple of Jesus, we teach that the essence of Christianity is to be nice. Where do we get such a notion? Certainly not from the actions of Jesus.

One of the hallmarks of Jesus' ministry was his constant attack on the status quo. He challenged it every time he could. He even went out of his way to upset the religious bullies of his time. He called them "white sepulchres" and by doing so attacked the very heart of their priesthood based on purity (Matthew 23:27 KJV). Jesus loved church leaders too much to allow them to remain such small persons. When Peter showed his displeasure over the impending death of his Lord, Jesus said to him, "Get behind me,

Satan" (Matthew 16:23). Jesus loved his disciples too much to let them miss one of the more important lessons of servanthood. Jesus was the man who said, "be compassionate as God is compassionate" (Luke 6:36). He had no desire to be nice because being nice has nothing to do with being Christian. Being nice is often nothing more than a lack of compassion for people. Let's explore what this means.

At one point, in a holy rage, Jesus entered the Temple with a large, metal-tipped whip and drove out the money changers. As he did, he quipped, "It is written, 'My house shall be called the house of prayer'; but you have made it a den of robbers" (Matthew 21:13). If we discover why Jesus responded to religious bullies this way, we will also discover why so many church leaders refuse to follow his example.

When Jesus cleansed the temple, he was in the Court of the Gentiles. This was the only part of the temple where Gentiles were allowed to worship. What ticked Jesus off was that the religious leaders were using the only place Gentiles could worship God as the place to sell their wares. What was to be a place of spiritual discovery and worship for the Gentiles was turned into an economic opportunity for the religious leaders. (Sound familiar?) The focus of the religious leaders was on themselves, not the spiritual vitality of the Gentiles. So he drove them out.

Therefore, thieves are those who do religious things for their own purposes. When we are doing things that only benefit those within the church, we become a den of robbers. When we say that we want it this way because it has always been this way, we are a den of robbers. When we focus on only the needs of our members, we are robbing the community of a chance to join us in our journey of faith. Such action is intolerable for people of compassion and love.

Church leaders are robbing people of their spiritual birthright when they allow dysfunctional people to sell their petty wares in the house of God rather than to proclaim release from bondage. We really need to get clear on this problem and do something about it. If we love people and if we want them to experience the love of God, then we will not ever allow the bully to rob others of their spiritual birthright. Anyone who knows how family systems work knows that the worst thing one can do with dysfunctional people is to give them more attention by giving into their every whim. Instead, tough love has to be applied. The compassionate thing to do is to hold them accountable for their self-centered actions, for in doing so they may begin the journey with God.

Jesus shows us what to do with people who do not want to grow spiritually. In training his disciples how to spread the word of God's love, he told the disciples to "shake off the dust from your feet" when they encountered people who did not receive them graciously (Matthew 10:14). Jesus loved people too much to let anything slow down the process of setting people free from their bondage, whatever it is.

People who would rather be nice than be Christian do not love enough. They do not have enough compassion. Instead, they are afraid of hurting someone or of being hurt. Remember, fear is the opposite of love. "Perfect love casts out fear" (1 John 4:18).

If we really cared about people, we would not allow them to bully others into submission. Instead we would want every person to feel free enough to express hopes and dreams, to stretch his or her wings, and to reach his or her God-given potential. If we really loved people, we would not base our decisions on whether or not people would like us for those decisions. Being nice or being liked is never a goal for followers of Jesus.

What does being nice accomplish in the church?

- More dysfunctional people
- Fewer spiritual giants
- An intimidated congregation

- An inability to spread the gospel
- Little hope of renewal or growth
- Discouraged church leaders

Being nice is not what Jesus wants from any of us. He wants compassion!

One of the basic lessons I'm learning as a consultant is that before renewal begins in a church or denomination, it is normal that someone has to leave or be denied. Almost every time a dying church attempts to thrive once again, someone tries to bully the leadership out of the attempt. And almost every time, if a turnaround is to take place, such persons are lost along the way because they are no longer allowed to get their way. When they can't get their way, they leave. Not even Jesus got through the journey with all of his disciples. Why should we expect to?

This does not mean that we should set out to intimate the bully or to kick people out of the church. It does mean that we care enough about the future of our church not to allow anyone to stifle its ability to liberate people from bondage or victimization. It means that we care enough about the bully that we will not allow the bully to intimate the church because we know the spiritual vitality of both the bully and the church is at stake.

Matthew 18 gives us a formula for dealing with the dysfunctional bully. First, an individual privately confronts the person with what he or she is doing and asks the person to stop. If this doesn't achieve positive results, two or more people are to confront the person. If this does not resolve the matter, the person is to be brought before the entire church. Listen again to the not-so-nice words of Jesus: "And if he shall neglect to hear them, tell it unto the church: but if he neglect to hear the church, let him be unto thee as a heathen man and a publican" (Matthew 18:17 KJV). In other words, withdraw from that person's presence, or in our case remove that person from office!

Never, ever, allow such a person to dictate the direction of the church.

The next time someone in your church attempts to intimidate or bully the church out of taking a positive step forward, go to God in prayer, and then get out the metal-tipped whip and drive that person out of the church—of course in love.[1]

Note

1. For more on how to do this, see William M. Easum, *Sacred Cows Make Gourmet Burgers* (Nashville: Abingdon Press, 1995).

APPENDIX 7

TURNAROUND LEADERS

Three out of four congregations today are either dying or stagnated. God is raising up turnaround leaders to change this picture. If they are to be successful in the turnaround, these leaders will learn two valuable lessons early in the process:

- A church won't be any healthier than its leadership.
- The turnaround usually results in spiritual warfare, so turnaround leaders develop a strong devotional life. Their deepening faith prepares them for the battle and the inevitable stress that comes from those opposed to change.

In the course of the turnaround, some normal stress points occur when:

- Controllers are pressured to leave office.
- Making the attempt either to change an existing worship service or begin an additional worship service.
- The pastor begins breaking the personal-chaplain mold and becomes an empowering leader.
- The transition begins to cost money.
- A desire for high commitment begins to encroach upon the entitlements usually afforded longtime members.

167

- New leaders make mistakes trying to implement the innovations.
- Churches with paid staff find that before the turnaround can happen, they must replace some long-term paid staff.

However, because of their spiritual depth, no matter how much stress occurs, effective turnaround leaders never take any conflict personally. There is an old saying, "When you swim with sharks, you better not bleed." Just keep in mind that they're not mad at you; they're mad at the changes you're making.

Turnaround leaders believe that taking part in fulfilling the Great Commission is a given for every congregation, not an option. Failure to understand this puts everything else in jeopardy. They don't ask the church if it wants to grow; that is a given.

Everything they do is geared around the turnaround: sermons, articles, conversations, studies, and so on. They live and breathe a thriving congregation. Pastors who fail at turnaround often spend too much time on solving problems and taking care of the membership.

Turnaround leaders are willing to pay an enormous price. The hardest ministry on the planet is turning around a church that does not want to be turned around (which is the vast majority of dying congregations). Three out of four pastors who attempt a turnaround lose their jobs because the pastor becomes the brunt of the anger. This is why pastors with high mercy gifts have the hardest time with turning around a dying church.

Turnaround leaders are usually team players. They always gather and nurture a team of called, gifted, and equipped laity before beginning the turnaround. Their goal is to empower and release this group into leadership positions. They know the task before them is bigger than the gifts they possess. Failure to gather this team is the number one reason turnaround leaders fail.

Turnaround leaders empower people rather than take care of people. Their first priority in life is to transform, equip, and empower people and communities. However, they know that part of transformation is also caring for people. In order to empower people you have to first love them. This is where the Great Commandment enters the picture. Turnaround leaders model grace without becoming a chaplain. They refuse to make people dependent on them. Instead, they develop systems and equip people to care for one another as directed in Galatians 6:2 instead of doing all of it themselves. In order for this to happen:

• Pastors have to give up most forms of ministry.
• Laity have to give up most areas of administration.

Turnaround leaders take the long view. Most turn-arounds take three to five years even though they usually begin the first day the new pastor arrives. In their diligent pursuit of their goal of transformation, leaders often act like two-year-olds and push until they are told no. Then they back off a while only to begin pushing again as soon as the dust settles. They take advantage of the situation anytime they can since they are convinced the church should grow. Turnaround leaders are able to articulate this vision so clearly that others want to be part of the turnaround team. One of the most important things a leader can do in the transformation process is to provide an atmosphere in which people feel as if it is okay to change. They know the pain of transformation must be overcome by the promise of the future. For example: Moses had to paint a picture of land with milk and honey in order for the people to see beyond the mud pits. One would think it would be easy to help people leave the mud pits of Egypt. Not so. They were not willing to leave until the promise of something better overcame the fear of leaving what is familiar, even if the journey is filled with pain. Developing and managing the vision is the most important aspect of transition. You don't manage the transformation process; you manage the vision. Most organizations are overmanaged.

Still, many set limits on how long they are willing to give the turnaround. Most studies show that if it hasn't begun within the first year, it won't happen. Beginning often means nothing more than gathering a few people who have caught the vision of a better day and helping them mature as Christians.

So before beginning the transformation process, do the following:

- Count the cost. Be prepared for conflict. It is rare to transform without conflict, especially if you are successful. You may lose some members and friends. You may lose your pulpit.
- Once you start, never under any circumstances stop the process. To blink leaves everyone in a mess. Those who are mad are still mad and those whose hopes you have elevated will be crushed and will lose faith in you.

THE SMALL DYSFUNCTIONAL CHURCH

In the past twelve years, I've consulted with more than 500 churches. In the beginning, most of these churches had fewer than 300 in worship. Nine out of ten of those churches were conflicted and dysfunctional in the way their members coexisted.[1] Now, I work mostly with much larger churches and less than one out of ten of them are conflicted or dysfunctional. (It seems the larger a church becomes, the less likely it is that it is ruled by conflicted and dysfunctional people or systems.)

Why is it that small churches seem to be more wounded than much larger churches? This section examines this phenomenon, its effects on leaders, and what can be done about it.

Salt of the Earth

The vast majority of the people in these wounded churches, small or large, are good people—the salt of the earth. They care deeply about their church and deserve much better than what they are getting out of their faith experience. Often, their lives are much fuller and happier when they are away from their church. I lament over so many wonderful people who are held captive in dysfunctional systems. If you are one of these folks, I encourage you to say "enough is enough." Don't remain resigned to mere contentment when you could have the ecstasy and joy of being part of a healthy, thriving community of faith.

The Issue Before Us

Understanding why smaller churches are more likely to be ruled by conflict and dysfunctional behavior than larger churches is critical to the future of established churches because of the number of small churches. It is easier for a few dysfunctional people to rule a small congregation than it is in a large congregation. The larger the church becomes, the easier it is to deal with conflicted people and to root out dysfunctional behavior in individuals or systems. Because of the size of the large church, a handful of people find it harder to intimidate the church leaders. In the small church a handful of people can get in control, intimidate the majority, and because the majority are good, caring people who do not want to hurt anyone, the church becomes dysfunctional and begins to decline.

Are large churches better than small churches? Of course not. Size is not the issue and we shouldn't get distracted by such silly thoughts. Size has nothing to do with good or bad. All churches have their problems. The only thing that matters in a church is whether or not people are growing in their relationship to God, self, and one another. One of the conditions necessary for churches to grow larger is the absence of major conflict and dysfunctional behavior.

To add insult to injury, unhealthy people tend to join unhealthy families. Unhealthy organizations soon become toxic. If not careful, healthy people become unhealthy when entering unhealthy systems. In order to survive in unhealthy systems, healthy people either have to change the system, leave the system, or become unhealthy. There are no other choices. And where do most of the young, energetic pastors begin their ministry? In small churches.

172

One question begs an answer: why do some pastors succumb to the dysfunctional system and some change the system? All large churches were once small churches. How did they avoid or overcome conflict and dysfunctional behavior? How did their leaders keep from becoming resigned to the way things used to be? These are questions we must now explore (for a detailed account of how to grow a small congregation into a thriving community of faith, see Jeff Patton's book *If It Could Happen Here . . .*).

Vision

A lack or loss of vision is the main reason churches become conflicted and dysfunctional. Neither the church nor the leadership has a calling worth dying for. They have lost their reason for being. People could not do some of the things they do to each other if their eyes were on Jesus and the mission of the church. Leaders would not tolerate a few intimidating the many if their heart burned to see the growth of God's kingdom.

Leaders must have a personal vision if the organization is to have vision. Just sitting down to write out a mission statement never results in a workable congregational document if the people drafting the document are not clear about the direction of their own spiritual journey. This is the primary reason most committees never come up with workable mission statements.

New church starts are often good examples of how vision disintegrates into maintenance and maintenance into despair. New churches usually begin with a passion to reach out to people who are not yet part of the church community and to welcome them into membership. After all, they will help pay the bills. Much of the people's efforts and thoughts are on reaching new people. Over time, the church begins to shift from outreach to maintenance. For example, if the vision for the new church was starting a church, then the vision soon morphs into the question "Are we big enough now?" If the answer is yes then the church enters a maintenance mode and the dysfunctional controller is now free to move in for the kill. The vision now shifts to the care and finding of the entitled members and people begin to say, "Before we go after any more new members we'd better take care of our members." And the decline begins because God will not honor a church that exists for its members.

However, if the vision of the new church is for growing the kingdom instead of starting a church, the vision never changes. The question then becomes "Does everyone in the area know God?" The size of the church is never the issue. The issue now is are we inviting, growing, and sending people out into the world to be leaven in society?

The presence of a burning, consuming vision that is worth dying for is what keeps any size church or any leader from becoming conflicted and dysfunctional. When such a situation arises, and it will, or when a small handful of people try to impose their will on the majority, and they will, the leaders stop such nonsense in its tracks because these people divert too much energy from the mission and that is unacceptable to people who have a vision worth dying for.

The Scriptures say that people without vision "perish" or "cast off restraint" (Proverbs 29:18). When this happens, pettiness creeps in and people are diverted from reaching out and begin to expect the pastor to take care of them. The only way some small churches experience the distractions that they do is because the people have nothing better on which to focus their time. Their lives are too small, so they become embroiled in mindless meetings that drain the soul. They walk the institutional hallways of decaying, joyless mausoleums, and they pick away at every little gnat in one another's eye.

Vision or purpose usually begin with the pastor. If the vision is lost, it is usually because the pastor has lost it or a new pastor has arrived who does not have a mission worth dying for. One of the major problems today is that too many pastors are dysfunctional and conflicted, especially in the smaller churches. Many pastors in small churches are either right out of seminary or have not been able to advance in the size of a group they are willing or able to lead. However, I have met many pastors in small churches whose hearts burn for more than just tending to the "inmates," but the inmates run the asylum. If you are one of these hopeful souls, I encourage you to rise up and say "enough is enough."

Note

1. By "dysfunctional" I mean that either the system or the individual is power-hungry to the point of being oppressive. I am not referring to the type of dysfunctional issues addressed by Twelve Step programs.